Church After Christendom

Stuart Murray

PATERNOSTER PRESS

First published in 2004 by Paternoster Press
09 08 07 06 05 04   7 6 5 4 3 2 1

Paternoster Press is an imprint of Authentic Media,
9 Holdom Avenue, Bletchley, Milton Keynes MK1 1QR, UK
and
P.O. Box 1047, Waynesboro, GA 30830-2047, USA

www.authenticmedia.co.uk

British Library Cataloguing in Publication Data
A catalogue record for this book is available from the British Library

ISBN 1-84227-292-6

Cover Design by FourNineZero
Typeset by WestKey Ltd, Falmouth, Cornwall
Print Management by Adare Carwin
Printed and Bound in Denmark by Nørhaven Paperback

Church After Christendom

'This is one of the very best books that I have read on the reshaping of the church for mission in our changed cultural context. As we have come to expect from Stuart Murray it is very well researched. It provides an informed guide to the key issues and will be invaluable in helping leaders discern which of the current trends have lasting value to reshape the church to come. Highly recommended.'

Graham Cray, Bishop of Maidstone and Chairman of the 'Mission-Shaped Church' Report

'The church in Britain is fortunate to have this pioneering work of Stuart Murray, challenging us to new ways of thinking about this post-Christendom era. *Church After Christendom* is a worthy successor to *Post-Christendom;* its breadth of knowledge and its perceptive questioning make it a must for national church leaders with a responsibility for shaping the Christian church of this century.'

Roger Whitehead, Executive Secretary, Group for Evangelisation

'With so much discussion (and not a little hysteria), these days about emerging church and the demise of the church as we have known it, it comes as a relief to find such a wise and measured reading of the post-Christendom landscape as Stuart Murray's. The future of the church in the West is surely in the kind of simple and sustainable churches he re-imagines, or else it has little future at all.'

Paul Goodliff, Head of Department of Ministry, Baptist Union of Great Britain

'In this book, a companion volume to his brilliant *Post-Christendom*, Stuart Murray asks all the right questions as he examines the changes happening in the church today and explores the church's future in the UK. Comprehensive yet accessible, and full of Murray's customary wisdom, this book is essential reading for all who believe the church can once again play a meaningful and vital role in people's lives.'

Vic Thiessen, Director of London Mennonite Centre

'Old points of reference are disappearing in this season of great transition. Stuart's book offers us no simplistic map that assures us as to what lies ahead, nor does he allow us to believe that life will ever be the same again. It is disturbing to every form of status quo but full of hope. Read it, be challenged, and enter into the honest dialogue that will help us journey to an unknown future.'
Martin Scott, Author of Gaining Ground and Impacting the City

'Stuart Murray holds a unique place among church planters, as a tested practitioner, theologian and mentor. Here he continues his helpful analysis of emerging and evolving churches, and offers hopeful suggestions of new ways to embody the gospel of grace.'
Patricia Took, Regional Minister, The London Baptist Association

'*Church after Christendom* is a crucial book for all those who are excited, agonized and serious about the present and future of the church in Europe. The author has an important hands-on overview of the church today and offers clear and focused light on the path ahead. It needs to be read with faith and hope, remembering that in other continents of our world the church is very much alive and growing. At the same time, it must be read with sobering realism, recognising that it may be the European church's call and destiny at this time to discover how church recovers and survives in an alien environment, and that our journey will be important for the church's future in those places where it is currently in numerical growth mode.'
Roger Mitchell, Church Planter and Church Consultant

To Neil, Viv and Noel

Contents

Series Preface

Many Christians have focused on the challenges of postmodernity in recent years, but most have neglected the seismic shifts that have taken place with the disintegration of a nominally Christian society. *After Christendom* is an exciting new series of books exploring the implications of the demise of Christendom and the challenges facing a church now living on the margins of Western society.

Post-Christendom, the first volume in the series, investigated the Christendom legacy and raised issues that are further explored in the books that follow. The authors of this series, who write from within the Anabaptist tradition, see the current challenges facing the church not as the loss of a golden age but as opportunities to recover a more biblical and more Christian way of being God's people in God's world. The series addresses a wide range of issues, such as social and political engagement, how we read Scripture, peace and violence, mission, worship and the shape and ethos of church after Christendom.

These books are not intended to be the last word on the subjects they address, but an invitation to discussion and further exploration. One way to engage in this discussion is via the After Christendom Forum hosted by the website of the Anabaptist Network:

www.anabaptistnetwork.com/AfterChristendom.

Church after Christendom
by Stuart Murray

How will the Western church negotiate the demise of Christendom? Can it rediscover its primary calling, recover its authentic ethos and regain its nerve? Stuart Murray surveys the 'emerging church' scene that has disturbed, energised and intrigued many Christians. He also listens carefully to those who have been joining and leaving the 'inherited church'. Interacting with several proposals for the shape the church should take as it charts a new course for its mission in post-Christendom, the author reflects in greater depth on some of the topics introduced in *Post-Christendom* and the practical implications of proposals made in that book. *Church after Christendom* offers a vision of a way of being church that is healthy, sustainable, liberating, peaceful and missional.

Coming next in the *After Christendom* Series:

Faith and Politics after Christendom: The Church as a Movement for Anarchy
by Jonathan Bartley

For the best part of 1700 years, the institutional church has enjoyed a hand-in-hand relationship with government. Indeed, the church has often been seen as the glue that has stopped political systems from disintegrating into anarchy.

But now for the first time in centuries, the relationship has weakened to the point where the church in the UK can no longer claim to play a decisive part in government. *Faith and Politics after Christendom* offers perspectives and resources for Christians and churches no longer at the centre of society but on the margins. It invites a realistic and hopeful response to challenges and opportunities awaiting the church in twenty-first century politics.

Acknowledgements

Working collaboratively is an Anabaptist instinct – inviting comments, questions, corrections and new insights on what has been said or written. Time pressures and a looming publishing deadline truncated this process to some extent, but I am grateful to several friends and colleagues for reading through some or all of the manuscript and offering various perspectives.

Where their comments overlapped and reinforced each other, I have responded with particular care and enthusiasm. The deficiencies in style and content that remain are my responsibility, not theirs. Thank you, my friends – Alan Kreider, Andrew Francis, Trisha Dale and Jeremy Thomson.

Some of the material, especially in Part One, I have presented over the past three or four years in various settings – especially in theological colleges and church leaders' conferences – and questions, challenges and responses I have encountered here have also helped shape this book. So my thanks also to several unnamed others.

Thank you, too, to my wife Sian. After several writing projects in the past two years, I have promised her that I will not start writing another book for at least twelve months! She too has read through the whole manuscript, chapter by chapter, and has helped me sharpen and clarify my thinking (and remove some comments that might unwittingly have caused offence).

I am grateful also to Robin Parry at Paternoster for commissioning not only this book but the *After Christendom* series, believing that the perspectives of various writers from the Anabaptist tradition might have a distinctive contribution to make to the way we think about church and mission at the start of the twenty-first century.

Finally, my thanks also to Neil MacLeod, Viv Lassetter and Noel Moules (to whom I have dedicated this book) – not only friends for many years, but my accountability group. Thank you for your friendship, support and counsel. Please remind me about not writing any more books for a while …

Part One

Shape

Prologue

Luke evidently regarded the conversion of Cornelius as a turning point in the mission and self-understanding of the early church. He recounts the incident twice: in Acts 10 he explains what happened and how Cornelius responded; in Acts 11 he retells the story from Peter's perspective and reflects on how the church in Jerusalem responded:

> The apostles and the believers throughout Judea heard that the Gentiles also had received the word of God. So when Peter went up to Jerusalem, the circumcised believers criticised him and said, "You went into the house of uncircumcised men and ate with them."
>
> Peter began and explained everything to them precisely as it had happened: 'I was in the city of Joppa praying, and in a trance I saw a vision. I saw something like a large sheet being let down from heaven by its four corners, and it came down to where I was. I looked into it and saw four-footed animals of the earth, wild beasts, reptiles, and birds of the air. Then I heard a voice telling me, "Get up, Peter. Kill and eat." I replied, "Surely not, Lord! Nothing impure or unclean has ever entered my mouth." The voice spoke from heaven a second time, "Do not call anything impure that God has made clean." This happened three times, and then it was all pulled up to heaven again.

Right then three men who had been sent to me from Caesarea stopped at the house where I was staying. The Spirit told me to have no hesitation about going with them. These six brothers also went with me, and we entered the man's house. He told us how he had seen an angel appear in his house and say, "Send to Joppa for Simon who is called Peter. He will bring you a message through which you and all your household will be saved."

As I began to speak, the Holy Spirit came on them as he had come on us at the beginning. Then I remembered what the Lord had said: "John baptised with water, but you will be baptised with the Holy Spirit." So if God gave them the same gift as he gave us, who believed in the Lord Jesus Christ, who was I to think that I could oppose God?'

When they heard this, they had no further objections and praised God, saying, "So then, God has granted even the Gentiles repentance unto life."

(Acts 11:1–18).

The significance of this incident, of course, is that, for the first time, a full-blown, card-carrying, pork-eating, uncircumcised Gentile had been converted, filled with the Spirit and baptised. This had profound and disturbing implications for the hitherto Jewish church. Soon, as reports arrived of many more Gentile converts, the Council of Jerusalem would debate these implications and Peter would refer back to this incident as the Council wrestled with issues of faith and culture.[1] But first he had to justify his taboo-breaking actions to the troubled Jerusalem church.

Cornelius had received the word of God (v. 1) and the Pentecostal gift of the Spirit (v. 15). What on earth had Peter been doing? The church had accepted the conversion of

---

[1] Acts 15:7–11.

Samaritans, but they were part-Jews. There was absolutely nothing Jewish about Cornelius: he was a Roman, an officer in the occupying army that was polluting the holy nation and oppressing the people. He was the enemy. Peter had eaten with an infidel in Caesarea, the enemy headquarters, and had declared 'the good news of peace through Jesus Christ'.[2]

This was truly shocking, although the apostles might have noticed resonances with things Jesus had said and done. There was his teaching about loving enemies.[3] There was that other centurion whose faith Jesus had compared favourably with most Jews.[4] And there was that commission to make disciples of all nations[5] – but surely that only meant finding Jews scattered through the nations?

The idea that Gentiles could become followers of Jesus was a profound challenge that led first Peter and then the church way beyond their theological boundaries, requiring them to re-examine their worldview and long-held convictions. This was harder for the church than for Peter. He had seen the vision; he had heard the voice from heaven; he had witnessed the Spirit coming on the Gentiles. The church simply had his report of what had happened.

Peter was clearly uncertain how this report would be received. He insisted God was responsible: God spoke to him (v. 7); the Spirit sent him to Cornelius' house (v. 12); the Spirit came on the Gentiles (v. 15); God gave them the gift of tongues (v. 17). Peter downplayed his own role: 'as I began to speak' (v. 15). He called on his colleagues to support his account (v. 12). And he posed the troubling question: 'who was I to think that I could oppose God?' (v. 17) – with the

---

[2] Acts 10:36.
[3] Matthew 5:43–48.
[4] Matthew 8:10.
[5] Matthew 28:18–20.

implicit warning that the church should be careful not to find itself opposing God.

How did the church respond? After all, though Peter was a respected apostle, he had a mixed track-record with a reputation for impulsiveness and the ability to be gloriously right or dangerously wrong.[6] The church voiced criticisms (v. 2) and raised objections (v. 18): they seemed more concerned about Peter eating with Gentiles than baptising them. But they listened carefully, discerned signs of God at work and accepted Peter's report, concluding: 'So then, God has granted even the Gentiles repentance unto life.' Is there a hint of uncertainty, of grudging acceptance? This would be understandable given the paradigm shift involved. Or is the tone one of wonder? Certainly they began to praise God for this unexpected development (v. 18).

Shifting Paradigms

The concept of 'paradigm shift' connotes significant dislocation in the worldview of an individual or community.[7] New evidence or experiences challenge our assumptions and presuppositions. Initially we feel disoriented and threatened and resist changes to our thinking or practice. But gradually, or quite suddenly, we learn to see the world in a new way, revising or reinterpreting our previous perspectives and embracing with varying degrees of enthusiasm a different understanding or vantage point.

---

[6] Matthew 16: 16–17, 22–23.

[7] The term was coined by Thomas S. Kuhn, *The Structure of Scientific Revolutions* (Chicago: University of Chicago Press, 1962). Its application to missiology is associated with David Bosch, *Transforming Mission: Paradigm Shifts in Theology of Mission* (Maryknoll: Orbis, 1991).

The end of Christendom and transition into post-Christendom in Western culture is a paradigm shift. Many Christians are resisting this shift and employing familiar tactics of defending the old paradigm, denying its demise, dithering on the cusp of a new era or delaying their commitment to this new reality. But Christendom is fading. We may grieve or celebrate its passing, but we cannot revive, restore or recover it. Post-Christendom is coming.[8]

The *After Christendom* series is grappling with the implications for the church and its mission of this paradigm shift. *Post-Christendom* investigated the earlier shift from pre-Christendom to Christendom, with its many ramifications through the following centuries.[9] *Church after Christendom* and future books in the series will probe more deeply into the Christendom legacy and the changes in mindset and action required of Christians in the strange new world of post-Christendom.

Church after Christendom focuses on the shape and ethos of the church. It develops themes from the first book, reflects on signs of turbulence in and around the churches as Christendom unravels, and considers attempts to recalibrate or reinvent the church. It identifies Christendom toxins that need to be purged from the ecclesial system and urges the recovery of perspectives and practices vital to sustain healthy churches after Christendom. It draws gratefully but critically on the praxis of pre- Christendom churches and dissident movements during the

---

[8] The focus in this book, and throughout the *After Christendom* series, is on Western culture, although we will interact at various points with the growing churches of the global South and expressions of non-Western Christianity in the West.

[9] Stuart Murray, *Post-Christendom: Church and mission in a strange new world* (Carlisle: Paternoster, 2004).

Christendom era. And, like the previous book, its conclusions and proposals are provisional, modest and exploratory as befits a period of transition from one paradigm to another.

Part One considers how church after Christendom might take shape. Some believe it can evolve from inherited forms of church; others suspect it will emerge from fresh expressions of church. Chapters 3 and 4 assess these claims and set them in a broader historical and global context. Before this, chapters 1 and 2 investigate two enigmatic but influential phenomena at the end of Christendom, which are already shaping our thinking and practice and may indicate priorities for church after Christendom: the relationship between believing and belonging, and the reasons why people join and leave churches.

Acts 11 represents an earlier paradigm shift. Although the issues we face are different, there are many connecting points between this passage and the challenges confronting post-Christendom churches. It is an encouraging story of risky missional engagement, accountable friendship, careful theological reflection and symbiosis between inherited and emerging expressions of church. It will be a helpful biblical reference point on the journey ahead.

1

Church After Christendom:
Belonging/Believing/Behaving

Belonging, Believing and Behaving After Christendom

His wife was a Christian and belonged to a church, but Ben was not a believer. He was a Jew and an agnostic. But over the years he watched and listened, developed friendships in the church, took part in various church activities and attended more regularly than many members. The church welcomed him and waited patiently. He imbibed their values and shared his own concerns, prayer requests and, finally, prayers. One day he called God 'Father'. Shortly before he died, eighteen years after first attending the church, he was baptised as a believer.

Mary was in her late fifties. She had never been to church before and she knew nothing about what Christians believed. She sat quietly at the back. On her way home she found herself 'speaking in this odd language'. The next day she returned various small items she had stolen from the office she cleaned and in the evening went to make peace with a neighbour to whom she had not spoken for twenty years. The following Sunday she returned to church, asking 'why am I doing these things?' She too was soon baptised as a believer.

Paul was in his twenties. He had left church because it did not connect with him spiritually or culturally and he was outraged by unacknowledged power politics in the congregation. He had always resisted the church's insistence that he should be evangelising friends and inviting them to church. He knew that they would find the services weird, trite and unappealing. But now he no longer had to worry about friends asking if they could attend church with him, the embarrassment had gone and all kinds of conversations were opening up. But he was unsure what he would do if any of them became Christians ...[1]

Belonging and Believing

The language of 'belonging' and 'believing' (and less often 'behaving') has become familiar in discussions about faith, church and mission. It offers helpful perspectives on issues facing churches after Christendom.

Researchers and sociologists, examining the relationship between what people believe and their participation in religious institutions, have identified two common positions – 'believing without belonging' and 'belonging before believing'. Some people do not belong to a church but identify themselves as Christians and hold beliefs that are more or less consistent with those who do belong. Others participate in church before they identify themselves as Christians or decide what they believe.

Many Christians seize on the first phrase to interpret their experience of friends and family members. They already know what researchers confirm and quantify. Many people believe in God, pray frequently, accept core Christian convictions and attempt to live by Christian values.[2] Some previously belonged to a church; others have only ever believed without belonging.

---

[1] These are true stories but the names have been changed.

[2] See, for example, David Hay, *Religious Experience Today: Studying the Facts* (London: Cassell/Mowbray, 1990); Martin

Mission strategists and church leaders are especially interested in the second phrase. Many parish churches have always functioned on the basis that parishioners 'belong' (and have certain legal rights) regardless of their beliefs. Elsewhere, however, those who wished to belong were expected to subscribe to certain beliefs. But churches that have historically applied a 'believing before belonging' approach report increasing numbers wanting to 'belong' before believing.

Many strategists encourage us to embrace this new paradigm. A key discovery of the Decade of Evangelism in the 1990s was that many people journey to faith gradually rather than suddenly. Churches that had previously expected 'crisis conversions' now recognised 'process conversions' as equally valid. This came as a relief to many Christians, especially in evangelical churches, where pressure to identify a definite conversion date prompted some to invent one to ward off suspicions they were not properly converted! The new paradigm has spawned 'process evangelism' courses[3] and has encouraged churches to become more welcoming, hospitable, inclusive and patient.

What factors have prompted 'belonging before believing' even in churches that previously required that belief preceded participation? Theological reflection on the relationship between belonging and believing appears to have followed rather than precipitated this change, so we must look to factors beyond the churches themselves. The most obvious are the cultural shifts signalled by the terms 'postmodernity' and 'post-Christendom':

---

[2] (*continued*) Robinson, *The Faith of the Unbeliever* (Crowborough: Monarch, 1995) and David Hay and Kate Hunt, 'Understanding the Spirituality of People who don't go to Church' (Nottingham University, 2000).

[3] See chapters 2 and 5.

- In postmodernity, people are suspicious of institutions and more interested in whether beliefs work in practice than whether they are theoretically true. So belonging before believing is necessary to test whether Christians live out in their communities what they claim to be true.
- In post-Christendom, knowledge of Christianity is limited; people need longer to understand and respond to the gospel. Furthermore, church culture is alien, so exploratory participation is safer than making a definite commitment.

Many emerging churches practise 'belonging before believing', considering this vital for engaging with a postmodern constituency. This approach attracts refugees from churches with firm boundaries that have resisted this paradigm shift. A 'centred-set' model of community is also popular, in contradistinction to the 'bounded-set' model operating in many inherited churches.[4] Centred-set communities represent a dynamic and flexible approach, allowing people to journey towards or away from a church without encountering fixed entry or exit points.

Discussions about the relationship between belonging and believing have highlighted significant missional and pastoral issues:

- The inadequacy of equating Christians exclusively with those who belong to churches.
- The importance of affirming the faith journeys of those whose conversion is gradual.
- The limitations of institutional membership models in contemporary culture.

---

[4] See chapter 3 for explanation of 'emerging' and 'inherited' churches.

- The challenge of building churches that faithfully and attractively incarnate the gospel they proclaim.
- The implications of prioritising core values over boundary maintenance.

These are issues to which post-Christendom churches must give careful attention.

Belonging and Believing Revisited

Interaction between belonging and believing is not restricted to these two familiar scenarios. Viewed through the post-Christendom lens, many variations are visible. To appreciate the complexity of post-Christendom we must examine further permutations of believing and belonging.

Believing and belonging

In pre-Christendom (roughly the first three centuries before the Christendom shift), believing and belonging were well integrated. Belonging was vital for believers as a deviant minority in an alien environment; and only believers would dare belong to an illegal organisation subject to persecution.

Although Christians shared their faith freely with friends and neighbours, church meetings were not open to outsiders: the danger of spies infiltrating the community precluded this. Those who expressed interest in Christianity explored this through a lengthy and demanding process known as *catechesis*. This explained what Christians believed and how they behaved. It also assessed whether enquirers were ready to take further steps towards belonging.[5] Catechists assumed no

---

[5] See Alan Kreider, *Worship and Evangelism in Pre- Christendom* (Cambridge: Grove, 1995) and *The Change of Conversion and the Origin of Christendom* (Harrisburg: Trinity Press, 1999).

familiarity with the Christian story or its values; and, since belonging meant participating in a counter-cultural community, learning what to believe and how to behave were both necessary. Neither belonging before believing nor believing without belonging was feasible. Growth in believing and belonging (and behaving) went hand in hand.

Required to believe and belong

In Christendom, everyone was required to belong to the church and believe what it taught. Dissent and non-attendance persisted for various reasons, but both attracted penalties. Belonging preceded believing, for infants were baptised into the church before they could even understand what to believe; but it was assumed they would grow up to believe what everyone believed.

However, as Christian beliefs were familiar, and mediated through multiple cultural symbols and an institution to which everyone belonged, churches gave less attention to catechesis. Rudimentary instruction, primarily dealing with liturgical and doctrinal issues, replaced the biblical and ethical teaching of pre-Christendom.[6] Christendom's version of Christianity was culturally conventional and imparted by osmosis rather than catechesis.

Christendom could be an oppressive culture, riddled with nominality and often with immorality, and the gulf between what church members were meant to believe and actually believed was often substantial (the same was true with regard to behaviour). But in an officially Christian society believing and belonging were mandatory.

---

[6] Everett Ferguson, 'Catechesis and Initiation' in Alan Kreider (ed.), *The Origins of Christendom in the West* (Edinburgh: T&T Clark, 2001), 267.

Daring to believe and belong

Those who dissented, espoused different beliefs and chose not to belong to the official church found themselves, like the early churches, on the margins – and in even greater peril (since the Christendom authorities were more efficient and persistent persecutors than their pagan predecessors). Consequently, the serious but voluntary belonging and believing that characterised the early churches reappeared in the medieval dissenting movements.[7]

Belonging but no longer believing

As Christendom unravelled between the eighteenth and twentieth centuries, many still belonged out of loyalty, social convention, family connections or inertia; but some no longer believed. They continued to attend for aesthetic or cultural reasons but resisted theological or spiritual development. Some became biblically illiterate or stymied in an adolescent belief system to which they could not seriously subscribe; others could not connect Christianity and the claims of modernity and retreated into dualism. Many ensured their church attendance had no practical influence on the rest of their lives.

Such attitudes may have been more or less prevalent throughout the Christendom era, but they became more visible as the social control exercised by the church weakened. This social churchgoing still persists but will surely disappear during the twenty-first century. Those for whom social factors remain influential are ageing and there is little evidence younger generations will continue to shore up declining congregations.

---

[7] See Murray, *Post-Christendom*, 324–39.

Believing but not belonging

But Christendom has unravelled in various ways. Another indication of its lingering influence is the proportion of the population who have never belonged to the church (except through church schools and christening or wedding ceremonies) but identify themselves as Christians and subscribe to Christian beliefs. Surveys over many years confirm this, although the content of what is believed varies considerably, with beliefs becoming more selective and syncretistic. Callum Brown notes:

> Though 74 per cent of people express a belief in the existence of some kind of God or "higher power", 50 per cent or fewer subscribe to the existence of sin, the soul, heaven, hell or life after death – while the numbers having specific faith in Jesus Christ as the risen Lord are so statistically insignificant that opinion pollsters do not even ask the question.[8]

Steve Bruce also insists that, though the proportion claiming Christian beliefs is higher than the proportion who belong to the churches, 'there is also considerable and consistent evidence that conventional religious beliefs are also declining in popularity ... there has been a steady decline in the popularity of Christian beliefs, which shadows the decline in church attendance.'[9]

Nevertheless, Christians have hailed each survey with enthusiasm as evidence that Christianity is alive and well in Western culture. Some suggest the churches should accept the validity of believing without belonging. Richard

---

[8] Callum Brown, *The Death of Christian Britain: Understanding Secularisation 1800–2000* (London: Routledge, 2001), 4.

[9] Steve Bruce, *God is Dead: Secularization in the West* (Oxford: Blackwell, 2002), 60, 71.

Thomas writes: 'Finding ways of speaking to the spirituality of a generation who do not come to church is not a matter of bringing them in, but of changing our understanding of the nature of Church itself.'[10] He even proposes a further category: believing *is* belonging – 'possibly the strongest form of belonging'.[11] Others, unconvinced by this interpretation, regard the surveys as stimuli to redouble efforts to persuade believers also to belong. Many such believers, however, are resistant, some regarding 'not belonging' as a virtue. Aspects of Christianity may be worth identifying with when completing a survey form, but the churches are generally not associated with these.

Grace Davie, who coined the phrase 'believing without belonging', detects a 'latent sense of belonging' and denotes the preferred option 'vicarious religion'.[12] Another suggestion is that many view the church like a fire station. They are glad it exists and are grateful for its expertise in the event of a fire. They may even be willing to pay for its services, but they will not convene on a weekly basis to celebrate its existence![13] Others distinguish 'nominal' and 'notional' Christians – the latter representing more tenuous believing and less likelihood of belonging. There are indications nominality is becoming notional Christianity, where ticking a survey form merely implies 'British' or non-member of another religion. As post-Christendom advances, both

---

[10] Richard Thomas, *Counting People In: Changing the way we think about membership and the church* (London: SPCK, 2003), vii.

[11] Thomas, *Counting*, 14.

[12] Grace Davie, *Religion in Britain since 1945: Believing without Belonging* (Oxford: Blackwell, 1994); *Europe: The Exceptional Case* (London: Darton, Longman & Todd, 2002).

[13] See www.elca.org/eteam/resources/NewEnvrnmtPostChristendom. htm.

categories will shrink, so we would beware investing false hopes in survey results.

This does not mean dismissing the beliefs and spiritual experiences of those who do not belong, and may never have belonged – any more than we should equate church membership with Christian faith. Such neat but simplistic categories were typical of Christendom but need not characterise post-Christendom. But we should not imagine a ready supply of non-belonging believers waiting for refurbished post-Christendom churches. A more creative missional strategy will be required.

Belonging but only partly believing

Belonging without believing may be diminishing, but some now belong who believe only part of what their churches teach. In modernity, Christianity was regarded as an integrated and coherent system inviting wholehearted belief or unbelief; but many in postmodernity affirm some beliefs but feel no obligation to accept everything.

Different churches cope with this pick 'n' mix tendency in different ways. Some find it threatening and exhort those who belong to endorse their whole belief system; some are relaxed about many aspects of what people believe but emphasise core beliefs and values; some adopt an almost entirely open approach with neither firm boundaries nor a definite core. Some welcome the challenge of dissenters and doubters, embracing the opportunity to reassess long-held convictions against biblical teaching, traditional understandings and contemporary approaches. Others are concerned that postmodern partial believing becomes disconnected from the Christian story and detracts from the integrity of Christian faith.

Believing but no longer belonging

Some believe who have never belonged; many others once belonged and still believe though they no longer belong. This is another form of 'believing without belonging', but the faith dynamics and attitudes of people in this category are very different from those who have never belonged.

There has been over the past several years an exodus of many who have belonged for years and were deeply committed members, who feel they can no longer belong with integrity. Most 'church leavers' still believe but no longer find belonging conducive to Christian discipleship. Chapter 2 will explore the reasons why they left and the implications for both leavers and churches.

Believing but belonging less intensely

Recent research indicates belonging no longer implies the same level of participation as it once did.[14] The term 'twicers' designated those who attended both morning and evening services each Sunday; it now describes those who attend services twice a month. Fortnightly and monthly participation is now common. Some are reluctant to take on responsibilities (especially regular responsibilities) in church life that previous generations would have welcomed. And many resist becoming church 'members' in a post-commitment culture or move easily and frequently between congregations and denominations.

Interpreting and addressing this widespread tendency is problematic. There are good reasons why many want to belong less intensely than their forebears: more complex

---

[14] See, for example, Peter Brierley, *The Tide is Running Out: What the English Church Attendance Survey Reveals* (London: Christian Research, 2000), 71ff.

family dynamics that place considerable pressure on Sundays; changing patterns of work that both require increased time commitment and offer vocational fulfilment many once found in churches; increased commuting times that preclude midweek participation; and involvement in community initiatives previously run by churches but now independent of them.

Some claim the Christendom model of belonging was rooted in a dualistic worldview and hindered Christians from incarnating the gospel beyond the congregation.[15] Less intense belonging is not a problem, therefore, but welcome liberation. However, such dualism likely applies more to the post-Enlightenment era than the sacral society of Christendom. The question this begs in post-Christendom is what level of belonging is needed to sustain incarnational discipleship in an alien culture.[16]

But many aspects of inherited church were designed for a different context in which churches were socially and culturally central. Marginal post-Christendom churches need not struggle to maintain programmes designed for a Christendom culture.

Believing and belonging intermittently

What happens to those who once belonged but leave even though they still believe? The next chapter will investigate this more fully, but we can note here (as a further expression of the believing/belonging nexus) that some leavers eventually return. This may be after many years and to a different kind of church from the one they left. But for many, though

---

[15] See James Thwaites, *The Church Beyond the Congregation: The Strategic Role of the Church in the Postmodern Era* (Carlisle: Paternoster, 1999).

[16] See further chapter 8.

by no means all, leavers the desire to belong finally overcomes their reluctance.

Another pattern is the tendency of some Christians to belong intermittently to several expressions of church. This may involve fairly regular involvement in two or more congregations; primary commitment to one church but frequent sampling of others; belonging to a dispersed Christian community; or participation in various informal Christian gatherings. A term some apply to this phenomenon is 'portfolio church'; others call it 'liquid church'.[17] Some interpret it as indicating the pernicious influence of consumerism; others regard it as inevitable and beneficial in a networking culture.

Belonging but not yet believing

How should we regard the acceptance by many churches, despite their theology and history, that many people want to belong before they believe? The creation of process evangelism courses and the more sensitive and hospitable attitude of these churches towards those some designate 'seekers' are welcome developments. If people want to explore Christianity by 'belonging' before deciding what they believe, churches can surely respond with integrity and patience.

But will 'belonging before believing' continue in an increasingly post-Christendom context? Perhaps it depends what we mean by 'belonging'. The process evangelism courses and revamped attractional strategies in which many are investing enormous hope may prove to be valuable but short-lived responses to this transitional period at the end of Christendom. The supply of 'seekers' may dry up.

---

[17] See Pete Ward, *Liquid Church* (Carlisle/Peabody: Paternoster/Hendrickson, 2002).

We will still need hospitable post-Christendom churches in which those who do not yet believe can participate as they explore faith. But 'belonging before believing' is actually the classic Christendom model. If we work with it in post-Christendom, we must beware Christendom temptations – waiting for people to come to us rather than going to them, downplaying conversion (whether through crisis or process) and underestimating the necessary induction process.

Believing but not yet belonging

As post-Christendom develops, some who have no connection with any church will come to faith through relationships with individual Christians. Incarnational forms of mission are emerging that no longer rely on attractional methods or people eager to belong before they believe. In these creative and courageous initiatives *centrifugal* mission is replacing *centripetal* mission. If 'belonging before believing' is applicable to such initiatives, the key is Christians 'belonging' within many neighbourhoods and networks, and building relationships through which 'believing' can begin.

Those who become believers may not assume 'belonging' is an important expression of 'believing'. They may not be averse to belonging, but church participation will not be automatic for them. But those who believe before they belong – even more than those who belong before they believe – will need more thorough discipling than most churches thought necessary in the last decades of Christendom. Post-Christendom converts, like pre-Christendom converts, will be joining counter-cultural communities with deviant values and beliefs rooted in an unfamiliar story. 'Process discipleship' courses may be more useful than process evangelism courses in post-Christendom churches.

Neither belonging nor believing

One category remains. In post-Christendom the vast majority of people will probably neither belong nor believe. Projections based on a continuation of current patterns of church decline suggest the Christian community will be much smaller by 2030 than it is today. Projections based on measurements of what people believe indicate believing without belonging will also diminish.[18] There is nothing deterministic about this, but honesty and realism are important if we are to respond faithfully and creatively to the challenges ahead.

What is less clear is the relationship between ceasing to believe and ceasing to belong. Stephen Green writes: 'Conventional wisdom and common sense suggest that people stopped going to church because they no longer believed what the churches taught them. Perhaps the causal mechanism was really closer to the opposite: they stopped believing because they stopped going.'[19]

At the heart of our response must be recalibration of the church as a cross-cultural missionary movement. We will return to this in chapter 5. Here we simply note that believing and belonging may be more integrally connected in post-Christendom than they have been since pre-Christendom. Belonging before believing may persist, but belonging without believing will surely disappear; and believing without belonging will be unsustainable in post-Christendom, where both believing and belonging will be minority pursuits of 'resident aliens' in a strange new world.[20]

---

[18] See further chapter 5.

[19] Stephen Green, *Religion in the Age of Decline: Organisation and Experience in Industrial Yorkshire, 1870-1920* (Cambridge: Cambridge University Press, 1996), 390–1.

[20] Terminology popularised by Stanley Hauerwas and William Willimon, *Resident Aliens: A provocative Christian assessment*

Degrees of Alienation

Alienation works in both directions. Christians in post-Christendom who accept their status as resident aliens will need to renegotiate how to be 'in the world' but 'not of the world'. This does not imply pietistic withdrawal from society but fresh thinking about *how* representatives of marginal churches with counter-cultural values engage in political and cultural debate and participate in local communities.[21]

Churches – whether understood as institutions, buildings or congregations – will be culturally alien in post-Christendom. They will be familiar as architectural legacies and their influence on the development of Western culture will be acknowledged (for post-Christendom implies a memory of Christendom). But the gap between churches as living faith communities and other people will be much wider than at present.

Considering even the current gap between church and culture, some suggest we are moving from a context where most people beyond the churches can be labelled 'de-churched' to one where more are actually 'non-churched'. Previously most people had at least limited knowledge of or connection with churches. But the 'non-churched' are rapidly overtaking the 'de-churched'. The Anglican report, *Mission-Shaped Church*, calculates they are currently neck and neck with 40 per cent non-churched, 20 per cent 'open de-churched', 20 per cent 'closed de-churched' and 10 per cent 'fringe attenders'.[22]

---

[20] *(continued) of culture and ministry for people who know that something is wrong* (Nashville: Abingdon, 1991).

[21] See further Jonathan Bartley, *Faith and Politics After Christendom* (Carlisle: Paternoster, forthcoming).

[22] *Mission-Shaped Church* (London: Church House, 2004), 37.

But 'if the groups are age-weighted, the de-churched are 25 per cent and shrinking and the non-churched are 65 per cent and growing.'[23] The absence from church of 96 per cent of British children suggests this proportional shift will accelerate.

The complex relationship between believing and belonging indicates we may need several categories to map the degrees of alienation from church experienced in late Christendom and post-Christendom:

- The *semi-churched* are those who have some connection with a church and occasionally participate in church activities but do not fully belong.
- The *de-churched* are those who have some familiarity with church but do not generally find churches attractive or amenable.
- The *pre-churched* are those with no prior experience of church, for whom church culture is alien and church language incomprehensible.
- The *post-churched* are those who have, for various reasons and often after years of involvement, decided to leave the church.
- The *anti-churched* are those with personal or ideological objections to church culture and maybe also to Christianity.

This language is problematic, not least in its omission of any reference to other faith communities and its Christendom-oriented assumption that 'churched' is the cultural

---

[22] (*continued*) 'Open' and 'closed' here refer to the receptivity of people to Christianity and the churches.
[23] Bob Hopkins and George Lings, *Mission-shaped Church: The Inside and Outside View* (Sheffield: Encounters on the Edge, 2004), 8.

norm, rather than a counter-cultural experience. And it categorises attitudes towards church rather than Christian faith (belonging rather than believing). But it offers a heuristic guide to the diverse attitudes of those with whom churches are hoping to engage. However, as post-Christendom advances, the first two categories will shrink dramatically. This has serious implications for churches whose evangelistic strategies concentrate on the diminishing number of semi-churched and de-churched people who might respond to attractional approaches.

In post-Christendom, incarnational cross-cultural mission strategies will be needed to reach increasing numbers of pre-churched and anti-churched people.[24] So we must stop relying on 'this-is-the-answer' and 'one-size-fits-all' evangelism packages. And our churches must be communities where those who believe can belong. Imaginative, courageous and culturally attuned churches will be needed to connect with those who are now distant and alienated from church.

Belonging, Believing and Behaving

Later chapters will examine many implications of developing such mission strategies and churches. Here we consider four further dimensions of believing, belonging and behaving in post-Christendom.

Centred-set churches

The 'centred-set' model is popular in many emerging churches and various strategists advocate it.[25] They contrast

---

[24] We will examine the post-churched category in chapter 2.
[25] Not all acknowledge their debt to Anabaptist missiologist, Paul Hiebert, *Missions and the Renewal of the Church* (Pasadena:

this favourably with the 'bounded-set' model, which has clear boundaries and maintains the integrity of a community by excluding any whose beliefs or behaviour are unacceptable. They present less often two other models: the 'fuzzy set', which has ill-defined boundaries and builds a more flexible community, although still ensuring coherence through boundary-maintenance; and the 'open set' where there are neither boundaries nor a definite centre.

The centred set appeals to churches wanting to encourage belonging before believing. It resonates with a postmodern culture where the notion of boundaries is uncongenial. However, unless all four models are considered, the centred set can be confused with either the fuzzy-set or the open-set models. This makes it less attractive to those who are concerned about the integrity of the church's beliefs and behaviour. If churches imagine that communities can thrive without core values or guiding convictions, the centred-set model can be dangerous.

If we advocate the centred set for church after Christendom, we must clarify what this does and does not mean. We can do this by contrasting it with ecclesial models from the Christendom era.

Christendom as a culture was a bounded set, maintained by strict control structures to ensure everyone within its boundaries believed and behaved correctly and by political or military action to defend it against those who did not belong. However, within the boundaries of Christendom the parish church was an open set – all parishioners were welcome, in many periods required, to attend. Questions were asked about behaviour or belief only in flagrant cases. The ensuing doctrinal and moral corruption provoked dissent from outraged Christians, some of whom formed

---

[25] (*continued*) Fuller, 1983) and *Anthropological Reflections on Missiological Issues* (Grand Rapids: Baker Book House, 1994).

alternative churches on the fringes of Christendom. Eventually it sparked the Reformation and, especially among Anabaptists and Calvinists, a more disciplined approach to community.

The open set is wonderfully inclusive but undisciplined. Without a strong centre, this cannot foster attractive or sustainable community. It survived in the church-friendly bounded culture of Christendom, but it will not do for post-Christendom churches.

Dissenters and some reformers introduced bounded-set churches, although they drew the boundaries differently. For Calvin, the boundary included the entire population in a reformed city; for Anabaptists and medieval dissidents, the boundary distinguished those who belonged to believers' churches from the outside world. Many evangelical and charismatic/Pentecostal churches today endorse and apply this approach.

The bounded set can certainly create and sustain communities, in which beliefs are clearly articulated, behaviour is prescribed and people know they belong. Bounded-set churches attract those who feel secure within boundaries and may be refuges for some beleaguered and disoriented Christians after Christendom. But churches that intend to operate as culturally attuned missional communities, rather than survivalist groups, may find this model restrictive and unappealing.

In the twentieth century, as Christendom waned and Christian beliefs and behaviour slipped further and further out of sync with contemporary culture, many churches adopted the fuzzy set. Although these had boundaries, those who belonged (or wanted to belong) could disbelieve many aspects of Christianity and behave in ways that were more consistent with contemporary norms than traditional values and expectations – but remain members of the church. There were limits to such deviations, but it was often unclear where these boundaries were.

Some found this liberal approach attractive – especially those who found bounded-set churches oppressive – but fuzzy-set churches have not thrived. This is an inherently unstable model, prone either to develop into the insipid and unsustainable open set or to revert surreptitiously to the bounded set, excluding those who challenge its culture and assumptions. Intolerant liberalism is as unattractive as other forms of intolerance. Churches after Christendom will need to do better than this.

Those who advocate centred-set churches must beware open-set or fuzzy-set models masquerading as such. Some churches that claim to be centred-set communities have not really understood the model. The centred-set church has distinctive features:

- It has a definite centre, comprising non-negotiable core convictions, rooted in the story which has shaped the community – and ultimately in Jesus Christ.
- This centre is the focal point, around which members of the community gather enthusiastically.
- Its core convictions shape the church and separate it from other communities in a plural and contested culture.
- The church expends its energy on maintaining the core rather than patrolling boundaries.
- Confidence in its core convictions frees the church to be inclusive, hospitable and open to others, who are welcome to explore the community.
- Those who 'belong' are moving towards the centre, however near or far away they currently are in terms of belief or behaviour.

- This is a dynamic rather than a static model, suitable for communities living towards a vision and missional churches that anticipate constant interaction with others.

Centred-set churches can be as inclusive as open-set churches, as relaxed as fuzzy-set churches and as committed to convictions as bounded-set churches.[26] They value the attractive elements of the other models but configure these differently. Centred-set churches encourage spiritual growth, theological investigation, intellectual honesty, receptivity to new ideas and new people, and a 'journeying' image of discipleship.

But they have a definite centre – from which a boundary emerges. Paul Hiebert explains:

> while centered sets are not created by drawing boundaries, they do have sharp boundaries that separate things inside the set from those outside it – between things related to or moving towards the center and those that are not. Centered sets are well-formed, just like bounded sets. They are formed by defining the center and any relationships to it. The boundary then emerges automatically.[27]

Churches with healthy centres are secure enough to welcome those who are exploring faith and searching for authenticity. They are relaxed, non-judgemental communities where questions, doubts, dissent and fears can be expressed, and where ethical issues do not preclude acceptance. They are inclusive without compromising,

---

[26] Some argue these core values effectively function as boundaries, excluding any who do not subscribe to them. But boundaries exclude people, whereas core values invite people to include or exclude themselves.

[27] Hiebert, *Anthropological*, 124.

communities with deep convictions that are nevertheless open to fresh insights, churches that allow and encourage critical engagement with beliefs and behaviour but test everything by its congruence with their founding story.

Is this model a legitimate way of describing the community that travelled with Jesus? He invited people to follow him, to become disciples and commit themselves to the vision and values of God's kingdom, but to remain open to others and to fresh insights rather than thinking they had arrived. Is it the model operating in Acts 11 as Peter and the Jerusalem church assess his experience in light of their core convictions and the life and teaching of Jesus? This principled flexibility allows them to weigh up Peter's report, welcome Cornelius and debate what counter-cultural discipleship might mean for Gentiles. Will post-Christendom churches find the centred-set model liberating and sustaining?

Conversion

Acts 11 records a double conversion – not only Cornelius and his household, but also Peter and the Jerusalem church. This conversion was transformational for Cornelius *and* for the mission of a hitherto Jewish church. Conversion involves a paradigm shift, a new way of seeing the world. Whenever mission involves evangelism rather than proselytism (imposing our norms), double conversions like this will occur.

Conversion is another biblical dynamic the Christendom shift has distorted. Sensitive Christians shy away from this terminology, aware that it connotes pressure to conform to particular beliefs and behaviour, and implies submission to the superior wisdom and righteousness of those already 'converted'. Conversion historically has often meant an imperialistic (and sometimes coercive) demand for obedience to the institutions, creed and ethical norms of a dominant church. Despite Christendom's demise, pre-packaged theology, condescending approaches and assumptions that converts will conform to the predilections of the evangelist have continued to plague evangelism. Conversion is unidirectional.

This history has bequeathed an unhelpful legacy. The evening before this chapter was written a woman who had asked for baptism reported that her adult son was coming to the service. But he had made it clear he 'did not want to be converted'! What was he afraid the church might try to do to him? He had no previous church involvement, and knew nothing of the history of Christendom, but he had a negative perception of conversion.

But the understandable aversion of Christians and others to conversion language must not preclude the recovery in post-Christendom churches of an authentic biblical emphasis on conversion. There are dangers here. Does 'belonging before believing' delay indefinitely questions of ultimate allegiance? Do process evangelism courses downplay the crisis of decisive commitment to Jesus Christ as Lord? Do centred-set churches imply no paradigm shift is necessary for those who would follow Jesus?

Christendom also distorted conversion by assuming everyone born into a 'Christian' society was automatically Christian. Conversion was unnecessary: all that was needed was 'confirmation' of what had been assumed since birth.[28] In post-Christendom this fiction is unsustainable. Even those born into Christian families and nurtured in the faith from infancy will face increasingly stark choices between social norms that are no longer remotely Christian and counter-cultural Christian discipleship.

---

[28] Indeed, 'conversion' was mainly used to signify entry into a monastic community. See Murray, *Post-Christendom*, 95.

Churches after Christendom will need a robust but chastened theology of conversion. Invitations to follow Jesus must be winsome rather than overbearing. And they must imply an ongoing journey of discipleship for those issuing as well as receiving such invitations. Conversion is a paradigm shift that stimulates news ways of thinking and living, not arrival at a predetermined destination. Conversion is multidirectional and lifelong.

This understanding of conversion changes the tone and content of evangelism. Peter's vision, the shock to his theology it represented and his encounter with Cornelius affected his message. His opening words – 'I now realise how true it is that God does not show favouritism but accepts those from every nation who fear him and do what is right'[29] – are humble, grateful and directed as much to himself as to Cornelius.

The testimony of the New Testament, pre-Christendom churches and later dissenting groups is consistent: conversion is crucial for building Christian communities. Post-Christendom churches will disavow the Christendom distortions and welcome the opportunity to recover a gracious but radical understanding of conversion.

Behaving

Conversion is about believing and belonging. It involves commitment to a story and a community. But it is also about behaving in ways that are congruent with this story and strengthen the life and witness of this community. 'Behaving' has intruded occasionally into this chapter, but it features less often in most conversations about church and mission than 'believing' and 'belonging'.

---

[29] Acts 10:34–35.

This is another Christendom legacy: providing people assented to the required beliefs and demonstrated they belonged by reasonably frequent church attendance, behaviour was investigated only if it became scandalous or socially damaging. Catechesis (now drastically reduced from its pre-Christendom expression) concentrated on doctrine and liturgy, not ethics. Ethical teaching tended to be derived from the Old Testament rather than the life and teaching of Jesus. Christian behaviour was equated with social conformity.

But church after Christendom dare not ignore 'behaving'. In a sceptical culture, faith must be lived if it is to be believed. In a culture moving away from both residual Christian values and distorted Christendom patterns, churches have new opportunities and responsibilities to incarnate the gospel authentically. This does not mean legalism or moralism (predictable but unhelpful reactions to the demise of Christendom), but counter-cultural churches that live out the attractive but provocative implications of the story they proclaim.

This may require a 'Christendom detox' that flushes out of the system attitudes and practices that hinder authentic discipleship. Another component may be a thorough induction process, whereby converts learn to follow Jesus. Catechesis is making a comeback. The Catholic *Rite of Christian Initiation of Adults* has been a major step towards this,[30] and several process evangelism courses also function as induction courses for converts (and refresher courses for others), exploring subjects catechesis traditionally covered. *Emmaus* is the most extensive, but *Alpha* began as a course for new believers rather than an evangelism course.[31]

---

[30] See www.ecatholic2000.com/rcia/rcia.shtml.

[31] See www.natsoc.org.uk/emmaus and www.alphacourse.org.

Post-Christendom catechesis will require more than induction courses – even courses that explore 'behaving' in far greater depth than any course currently available. It will mean rehearsing the 'big story' and core values of the community, so these are deeply internalised. It may include a form of cultural exorcism, confronting the norms of a cynical, individualistic, patriarchal, consumerist culture, built on global injustice and sustained by institutional violence. And it will involve mentoring, apprenticeship and accountability processes.[32]

This does not mean reinventing bounded-set churches. Believing, belonging and behaving are not separate stages but different dimensions of the journey on which all followers of Jesus are pilgrims. Progress in one dimension precipitates progress in others. Belonging influences what we believe and how we behave. Believing changes our behaviour and deepens our belonging. Behaving enhances our identity with the community and undergirds what we believe. Post-Christendom churches will be messy communities where belonging, believing and behaving are in process rather than neatly integrated.

Learning to behave as Christians is an aspect of conversion and similarly lifelong and multidirectional. Induction offers learning opportunities for all involved: questions new converts raise challenge the assumptions and behaviour of older Christians. The conversion of Cornelius put new issues on the agenda for Jewish Christians. Initially they pondered what behaviour to require of Gentile converts and devised a provisional answer (Acts 15: 5, 19–20). In due course this would help them differentiate between cultural norms and ethical behaviour applicable to all

---

[32] See further chapter 6 and Alan Kreider, 'Initiating Attractive Christians: Lessons from the Early Church', *Anabaptism Today* 36 (2004), 2–7.

Christians. Post-Christendom churches will relish the opportunity *both* to induct converts into the story of Jesus and the values of his upside-down kingdom *and* to receive their help in identifying areas of inconsistency and compromise in their own communities.

Membership

In centred-set churches where belonging, believing and behaving are in flux, is there any room for a category of 'members'? Is there any difference between 'belonging' and 'membership'?[33]

As Steven Croft notes, 'member' derives from *membrum* 'which means "a limb or part of the body" ... a very strong and close way of belonging.'[34] But 'member' today sounds institutional and many find this terminology unhelpful. In a post-commitment culture, membership (however defined) is problematic, not only for churches, but for many organisations. Post-Christendom churches will need categories and terminology that are culturally attuned – but also counter-cultural.

The single category of membership (differentiating members from non-members) is unwieldy, static and exclusive in centred-set churches, where more nuanced, dynamic and inclusive concepts are operative. Post-Christendom churches may need various categories of belonging:

- Flexible and relational, rather than institutional, categories.

---

[33] *Post-Christendom* included a brief discussion about membership and the terminology used to indicate belonging. See Murray, *Post-Christendom*, 308–10.

[34] Steven Croft, *Transforming Communities: Re-imagining the Church for the 21st Century* (London: Darton, Longman & Todd, 2002), 129.

- Categories that encourage expressions of commitment consistent with changing beliefs and behaviour.
- Inclusive rather than exclusive categories that refer to core values rather than boundaries.
- Categories coherent with our identity as pilgrims who respond haltingly but hopefully to Jesus' call to follow him.

John Drane's proposal was mentioned in *Post-Christendom*:

[a] stakeholder model, in which there could and would be a place for diverse groups of people, who might be at different stages in their journey of faith, but who would be bound together by their commitment to one another and to the reality of the spiritual search, rather than by inherited definitions of institutional membership.[35]

But centred-set churches need custodians of their story and values. Inclusivity and open-ended belonging without core maintenance is unsustainable and dangerous, as membership-averse emerging churches are discovering. Other emerging churches are reconfiguring monastic patterns that establish a core community and allow for various stages of commitment to their core values. Nigel Wright, affirming diverse forms of belonging, warns that a church is 'unlikely to endure unless at its core there are those who commit themselves on a *covenantal* basis'.[36] He proposes an open 'community membership' and a 'core membership' open to those who accept its demands.

---

[35] John Drane, *The McDonaldization of the Church: Spirituality, Creativity, and the Future of the Church* (London: Darton, Longman & Todd, 2000), 159.

[36] Nigel Wright, *New Baptists, New Agenda* (Carlisle: Paternoster, 2002), 79.

This is where baptism intersects centred-set ecclesiology. Baptising infants assumes an open set and is inappropriate for centred-set churches. Baptising those who, like Cornelius, respond to the gospel fits much better. Baptism marks the point at which someone covenants to believe in Jesus, belong to the church and behave in ways that are consistent with its core values.

The complex relationship between belonging, believing and behaving will reappear in subsequent chapters. We turn next to the dislocation between believing and belonging evident in the stories of many Christians who have left churches in recent years. If this flow is not stemmed, discussions about post-Christendom churches may be academic.

2

Church After Christendom:
Comings and Goings

Church after Christendom is shrinking. The net result of the various permutations of believing and belonging is that, however we calculate or interpret belonging, fewer people now belong to the churches. Nothing anyone has proposed to reverse this decline has yet succeeded, though several measures may have slowed it down. The figures and prospects are discouraging. Unless the situation changes, in Western culture there will *be* no church after Christendom.

People respond to this scenario in much the same way as they react to suggestions that Christendom is dying.[1] Some are in *denial* and continue to believe that doing more enthusiastically, prayerfully and persistently what we are already doing will turn the tide, or that divine intervention will rescue us. Some *defend* current structures and strategies, blame cultural changes and anticipate eventual recovery if we remain faithful and do not panic. Others *dissociate* themselves from this analysis, claiming that their church, stream or denomination bucks the trend and has a bright future.

---

[1] Murray, *Post-Christendom*, 206–16.

Joining and Leaving

The picture, of course, is mixed. What we see depends on where we stand and how far we look beyond our own situation. It has been estimated that 25 per cent of churches grew numerically in the 1990s. Some denominations and networks are holding their own or growing. We are planting churches and planning more. But many churches are losing members and those members who remain are ageing. Many more churches closed in the 1990s than opened. Some networks are disintegrating and, if nothing changes, some denominations will soon be non-viable. Encouraging instances of growth do not offset the overall trend of decline. In the 1980s and 1990s, 1.6 million people joined churches, but 2.8 million left them.[2]

There are signs that this scenario is prompting creative and courageous action and also careful analysis. We need both. The situation is too urgent to delay action indefinitely while researchers collect and process information; but it is too serious to rush headlong into schemes and programmes without understanding the context, the current situation and the challenges we face. In chapter 3 we will investigate activities taking place on the margins of the church, asking if emerging churches are pointing the way forward. In this chapter we will interact with research and analysis that offers insights into where we are and what we might do.

Churches are shrinking both because fewer people are joining and because more are leaving. To address this situation we need to know more about the joiners and leavers. Who are joining the churches, and why? Who are leaving the churches, and why? Are there some churches that people are joining and others that people are leaving, or are there churches where different people are joining and leaving? We need to know more about both the front doors

---

[2] Brierley, *Tide*, 84.

and the back doors of our churches. We can address church decline in two ways: by encouraging more people to join and by encouraging fewer to leave. So we need to listen to the joiners and leavers: what makes churches worth joining, and what prompts people to leave?

We need to listen carefully, sympathetically and critically. Those who remain and resent them leaving find listening to leavers is difficult. It is especially difficult for church leaders. The leavers' criticisms of the churches they have left can be sharp and distressing. But we must hear and face their criticisms if we are not to watch many more exit through the back door. However, people leave churches for many reasons and we must beware excessive self-flagellation. Indiscriminate blaming of churches is no more legitimate than indiscriminate blaming of leavers. It is easier to listen to joiners, but here too we must be careful how we listen. People join for many reasons and in various ways. We must also identify who is not joining and recognise the cultural chasm between many churches and contemporary culture.

We can investigate why people join churches by considering three pieces of research conducted over the past fifteen years. These focus primarily on evangelism and how people find faith, rather than why they joined churches, but there is much overlap. In 1992 John Finney wrote *Finding Faith Today*, summarising the results of interviews with over 500 people who had made a 'public profession of faith' during the previous year. Finney urged his readers to 'honour and learn from those who are beginning the journey of faith'.[3] In 1996 Robert Warren's *Signs of Life* presented a mid-term assessment of the Decade of Evangelism.[4] And in 2003

---

[3] John Finney, *Finding Faith Today* (Swindon: Bible Society, 1992), 110.

[4] Robert Warren, *Signs of Life: How Goes the Decade of Evangelism?* (London: Church House, 1996).

Mike Booker and Mark Ireland evaluated contemporary evangelistic strategies in *Evangelism – Which Way Now?*[5] These books contain helpful insights for our purposes.

Several books about church leaving have also appeared in the past decade, based on extensive or intensive research and conversations with leavers. These must be cross-referenced: although they present a coherent picture, different researchers emphasise different issues and may in some cases be describing different kinds of leavers. Alan Jamieson's *A Churchless Faith* and *Journeying in Faith* have been very helpful, both to researchers and to those who recognise themselves or their friends in his writings.[6] But not all leavers fit the profile he presents. Philip Richter and Leslie Francis offer a more comprehensive analysis in *Gone but not Forgotten.*[7]

But we should also compare these areas of research. Is there any common ground? How do the reasons joiners give for joining relate to the reasons leavers give for leaving (sometimes, it seems, the same) churches? Are some churches effective at wooing joiners but ineffective at retaining leavers, and vice versa? Can churches be effective at both? If we can discover what encourages people through the front door and what might discourage people from leaving through the back door, we will be in a better position to

---

[5] Mike Booker and Mark Ireland, *Evangelism – Which Way Now?: An Evaluation of Alpha, Emmaus, Cell Church and Other Contemporary Strategies for Evangelism* (London: Church House, 2003).

[6] Alan Jamieson, *A Churchless Faith: Faith Journeys Beyond the Churches* (London: SPCK, 2002) and *Journeying in Faith* (London: SPCK, 2004).

[7] Philip Richter and Leslie Francis, *Gone but not Forgotten: Church leaving and returning* (London: Darton, Longman & Todd, 1998).

identify aspects of church life that will sustain post-Christendom churches.

Surprisingly, these two areas of research are rarely brought together. Researchers are generally interested in what is happening at the back door or the front door but not at both doors.[8] But to understand the dynamics of post-Christendom churches and the issues we face, we need a more comprehensive picture of the comings and goings. Cross-referencing these areas of research reveals interesting information and provocative areas of agreement.

Through the Back Door

Approximately 2,000 people leave British churches every week. Some transfer to other churches, either because they have moved home or to a different church in their own locality. Some die, transferring from the church on earth to the great cloud of witnesses who spur on the present generation to faithful perseverance (Heb. 12:1). But 1,500 people a week leave churches for other reasons.[9] It is with these leavers we are mainly concerned here – although there are issues we should briefly note in relation to other leavers:

- In ageing congregations, those who die after decades of belonging are often not, as in previous generations, replaced by new and younger members. The *age profile* of congregations and denominations is a key factor in projections of future viability.
- Many who transfer from one church to another also change denomination, not because of

---

[8] Although Finney wrote the foreword to Richter and Francis' book, commending it for complementing his research.
[9] Richter and Francis, *Gone*, 2.

denominational preferences but because
denominational allegiance is irrelevant to them.
Other factors influence their decision.
Post-Christendom churches will operate in a
post-denominational situation. Denominations and
other translocal networks will persist (though
current structures may become unsustainable), but
few will be ideologically or emotionally attached to
them.

- The frequency and apparent ease with which
  Christians move from church to church indicates the
  influence of a *post-commitment* culture with its
  prevailing values of individualism and consumerism.
  These values threaten the well-being or even survival
  of political organisations, voluntary associations,
  community groups and other institutions that
  depend on regular participation and faithful
  membership. Postmodern cynicism, distrust of
  institutions, self-fulfilment as the primary good and
  spectatorism discourage commitment and
  perseverance. Church after Christendom may need
  to nurture counter-cultural reflexes if it is to thrive.
- Many apparently successful churches grow primarily
  through transfers from other churches, rather than
  through effective evangelism. Martin Robinson
  comments: 'what such churches have actually
  learned is not how to become significant missionary
  congregations but how to attract Christians from
  other churches more effectively than other
  congregations.'[10] Churches that rely on *transfer
  growth* are not pioneers of church after

---

[10] Martin Robinson and Dwight Smith, *Invading Secular Space:
Strategies for Tomorrow's Church* (London: Monarch, 2003),
30.

Christendom. They may obstruct the development of
strategic mission initiatives and the effective
deployment of Christians.

But many people have not transferred from one church to
another – they have left the church altogether. A recent esti-
mate is that a million Christians no longer belong to
churches and that this is the fastest growing part of the
Christian community. There is heavy traffic through the
back door.

Leaving the church

These are the post-churched.[11] Many belonged for years or
decades and were deeply committed, involved in mission
and ministry, exercising leadership, evangelising their
friends and neighbours, praying and working for social
transformation and church renewal, worshipping enthusiastically and giving generously of their time, money, homes
and lives. They were (and some still are) our friends. We
know why some left; others are not quite sure themselves.

Throughout history people have left churches. Even in
the New Testament we read of some who 'went out from
us';[12] and through the centuries, even though belonging was
compulsory, people left quietly or with fulminating pro-
tests. The churches regarded leavers as heretics, apostates,
schismatics, backsliders, the 'lapsed' or 'antichrists'.[13] 'For
if they had belonged to us, they would have remained with

---

[11] Some designate them 'de-churched', a term chapter 1 used for
those who are familiar with church but were never as deeply involved as the post-churched. The boundaries are indistinct, but
conflating these groups may cause confusion.

[12] 1 John 2:19.

[13] 1 John 2:18.

us; but their going showed that none of them belonged to us.'[14] The fault lay with them and required no soul-searching by the church.

But the demise of Christendom has precipitated an accelerating exodus, as changing cultural expectations and the church's diminishing status have made leaving easier. Some Christendom vestiges (both attitudes and practices) have also prompted some to leave, dismayed or outraged by their persistence within the churches.[15] Responses to this exodus have changed. Many still prefer to find fault with those who leave, but conversations with leavers – in formal research projects, pastoral visits and multiple informal settings – have revealed that this is not the whole story. Many leavers have departed reluctantly, after months or years of struggling to remain:

- Some leavers have lost their faith and walked away from Christianity as well as from church; but most have left because church is no longer nurturing their faith, engaging with their questions or helping them mature as Christians.
- Some leavers, unwilling to repent of behaviour they acknowledge to be sinful, have disembarked rather than participating hypocritically; but many have left because they could no longer stomach the sinful attitudes, destructive behaviour and nauseating self-righteousness of their church.
- Some leavers have fallen out with people and have departed refusing to be reconciled; but many others have found the political manoeuvring, back-biting and institutional incapacity to handle conflict responsibly more than they could stand.

---

[14] 1 John 2:19.
[15] See Murray, *Post-Christendom*, 189–91, 200–3.

- Some leavers were disillusioned by the fall from grace of respected leaders; but many left only because of the way such situations were mishandled or covered up.
- Some leavers allowed work, family, study, sports, hobbies or other activities to intrude on and eventually replace church involvement; but others have left because church offered no resources for living as Christians beyond its narrow sub-culture.
- Some leavers were embittered by trauma, divorce or redundancy, the death or illness of family members, struggles with singleness or sexuality; but many found neither the pastoral support nor simplistic theology of their church adequate for their pain, loneliness and questions.
- Some leavers have almost carelessly abandoned church when moving home, changing job or facing other new circumstances; others, finding the demands of the church unrealistic and burdensome, left to avoid burn-out and preserve their sanity.
- Some leavers lost heart after years of struggle in a declining congregation that was making no impact on society; others felt betrayed by unrealistic expectations and unfulfilled prophecies for which nobody accepted responsibility.

Reasons for leaving

People leave churches for many reasons. Each story has unique features, and often various factors combine to precipitate leaving. But researchers have identified several clusters of reasons. Michael Fanstone suggests people leave because of personal pain, difficulties with leaders, the apparent irrelevance of church and failing to encounter

God.[16] Philip Richter and Leslie Francis work with eight categories: loss of faith, changing values, stages of faith, changes and chances, family issues, burn-out, disappointed expectations and a lack of a sense of belonging. They discovered that, while some leavers blamed the church, 'other church leavers ... make it quite clear that it is *not* the church that is at fault in their case.'[17]

For significant numbers of Christians inherited forms of church are simply not working. Many have already left and more will leave in the coming years; others feel similarly about church but remain out of loyalty, habit or inertia. The exodus is impacting all denominations and many congregations – including new and growing churches and networks. Leavers include deeply committed Christians, many of whom were at the heart of their church and often in leadership. Some have abandoned their Christian faith; but many have abandoned only church. Some are uninterested in returning; others miss church, despite everything, and want to find a way back. Some are bitter and disillusioned, critical of the church and not expecting anything to change; others long for authentic church life and hope something new may emerge. The reasons why Christians leave churches are not secret. Several researchers have documented these reasons and they are easily accessible. But many churches prefer to ignore these reasons and attribute leaving to other causes, rather than facing the challenges they present.

Researchers in other Western societies confirm British findings and note other factors. In the USA William Hendricks lists reasons for leaving given by those he interviewed in 'exit interviews'. The reasons he discovered

---

[16] Michael Fanstone, *The Sheep that Got Away* (Tunbridge Wells: MARC, 1993).
[17] Richter and Francis, *Gone*, 120.

include: growing distrust in the institutional integrity of the church; lack of authenticity in relationships; utter boredom with church services; antipathy towards formulae and pre-packaged Christianity; disillusionment with hype; weariness with programmes; rejection of prosperity theology; the effect of gossip and betrayal; burn-out; failure to find God in times of crisis; and churches that fail to equip their members for daily life. Some women also expressed resentment at male domination in church culture.[18] Peter Kaldor reports that Australians leave church when they move home or get married; when they disagree with the church's theology; when their needs change; when they are unhappy with the style of the church; and when they experience conflict with church leaders.[19]

New Zealander Alan Jamieson's books have been particularly influential in recent years. Some aspects of his research do not translate easily into the British context (especially lumping together evangelical, Pentecostal and charismatic churches under the acronym EPC, which does not suit the less homogeneous British churches). But his analysis of church leaving has struck a chord with many Christians – in and no longer in church – not least because his books give voice to leavers themselves.

A Churchless Faith is based on in-depth interviews with 108 leavers and 54 church leaders. Among its most significant findings are the following:

- A typical 'leaving process' consists of four stages: first doubts, seeking and weighing alternatives, negotiating turning points and developing a new sense of identity.

---

[18] William Hendricks, *Exit Interviews* (Chicago: Moody, 1993).
[19] Summarised in Heather Wraight (ed.), *They Call Themselves Christians* (London: Christian Research/LCWE, 1999).

- There is a serious mismatch between the reasons leavers give for leaving and explanations church leaders offer (though counsellors and theological lecturers interpret leaving in ways that are much closer to leavers' reasons).
- The factor most church leaders fail to recognise is 'changing faith dynamics': leavers conclude that church no longer provides spiritual nourishment or stimulus.
- Many leavers continue their spiritual journeys. Four stages in these journeys can be detected (though not all progress through all these stages): disillusioned followers, reflective exiles, transitional explorers and integrated wayfinders.
- Churches can become more 'leaver-sensitive', but many leavers will discover resources for their ongoing journeys in 'post-church' groups.

The understandable enthusiasm with which many, especially post-evangelical and post-charismatic Christians, greeted this book should not preclude some questions and concerns. How typical are the interviewees? They are very articulate, mostly highly educated and mainly ex-leaders; almost none have lost faith altogether and many have re-connected with other Christians. As the research targeted EPC churches, it would be unfair to criticise it for dealing exclusively with leavers from such churches, but we should not assume those who leave other churches are on similar journeys.

Another concern is Jamieson's largely uncritical dependence on James Fowler's 'faith development' model[20] and his

---

[20] See James W. Fowler, *Stages of Faith: The Psychology of Human Development and the Quest for Meaning* (San Francisco: Harper & Row, 1981).

interpretation of leavers' experience primarily in terms of transition between stages three and four of this model. This interpretation is illuminating for both leavers and EPC churches, but sometimes it seems too facile an explanation of the stories interviewees told. Some writers have also questioned Fowler's model along these lines, as well as criticising it for overemphasising cognitive aspects of faith and for being individualistic, unidirectional, male-oriented, elitist, Westernised, value-laden and lacking room for conversion experiences.

There is no doubt that difficulties arise when Christians perceive a mismatch between the spiritual focus or maturity of their church and the stage they have reached on their own journey.[21] Many EPC churches do not encourage or provide resources for those who yearn to move beyond definite but simplistic answers and explore other approaches to worship, theology, ethics or spirituality. Other leavers, however, are alienated by churches that are reluctant to move beyond open-ended questions to deeply held convictions and abandon responsibility for mission in favour of meeting the spiritual needs of existing members.

But faith development issues are by no means the only factors in people leaving churches. The poignant stories Morris Stuart tells offer important correctives, as does a leaver's letter that constitutes the epilogue to his book.[22] Most leavers he introduces are disillusioned by the failure of their churches to engage radically with issues of social justice rather than their failure to encourage and resource faith development. Meic Pearse and Chris Matthews note three recurrent issues: leavers are dissatisfied with the style of

---

[21] Other researchers use Fowler's model, though more critically. For example, Richter and Francis, *Gone*, 53–64.

[22] Morris Stuart, *So Long, Farewell and Thanks for the Church?* (London: Scripture Union, 1996).

meetings, disagree with leaders and are disgruntled that their needs are not met.[23] While few of Jamieson's interviewees had abandoned their faith, 16 per cent of adult respondents in Richter and Francis' survey said 'loss of faith' was the precipitating reason for leaving church; 22 per cent pointed to life changes; interestingly, only 1 per cent identified faith development issues.[24] Richter and Francis conclude: 'unfulfilled expectations, loss of faith, and the changes and chances of life ... constitute the main causes associated with church leaving' and insist: 'a multidimensional approach to church leaving cannot be avoided.'[25]

Provided we do not regard them as a full account of why people leave (even EPC) churches, Jamieson's books are revealing and stimulating, not least because of his sympathetic approach and the challenges he presents to the churches. *Journeying in Faith* employs the images of the desert and 'the dark night of the soul' to explore the spiritual experiences of leavers. This book offers further insights into church leaving: some people who are still physically present in church have left spiritually and emotionally, so should be included as 'church leavers'; the way churches handle difficulties in church life (such as moral failures by leaders) is more critical than the difficulties themselves; and leavers are deeply critical of the ways their churches understand and practise evangelism.

Responding to leavers

For those who remain convinced that the church, for all its weaknesses, is crucial in the missionary purposes of God,

---

[23] Meic Pearse and Chris Matthews, *We must stop meeting like this ...* (Eastbourne: Kingsway, 1999), 22–4.
[24] Richter and Francis, *Gone*, 137.
[25] Richter and Francis, *Gone*, 141, 120.

this haemorrhage of leavers represents a strategic challenge. For those who doubt that believing can be sustained indefinitely in post-Christendom without belonging, it represents a pastoral crisis. Losing thousands of Christians through the back door saps the energy and enthusiasm of churches. Why hold open the front door if those leaving outnumber those who join – some of whom we will damage or disappoint so badly that sooner or later they will become leavers? To change the image, we need to plug the hole in the bucket before we pour in more water!

Post-Christendom churches, for the sake of both pastoral care and mission, will want to develop remedial and preventative responses to this situation.

- *Pursuing*. Researchers report the surprise of many leavers that nobody asked why they had left. Many who had been deeply involved in church for years were simply allowed to slip away. Whatever the explanation (negligence, fear, embarrassment?), this pastoral failure exacerbates the pain leavers feel and confirms their decision. Many have no intention of returning but would have welcomed a chance to explain why they were leaving. Others have not ruled out returning, but are discouraged by the church's failure to pursue them. 'Churches that fail to follow up leavers within six weeks of their leaving are missing an important opportunity.'[26]
- *Listening*. The dominant Christendom church was often arrogant and assumed leavers were at fault. This attitude evidently persists. Jamieson reports: 'Very few church leaders talked of incidents where they had sat down with leavers from their own churches, or any other church, to hear people's

---

[26] Richter and Francis, *Gone*, 145.

reasons and learn from them.'[27] Post-Christendom
churches will want to listen carefully and humbly to
leavers, ready to learn from them and respond to
their concerns. Leavers have insights and
perspectives that can sensitise churches to issues
that hinder their witness and community life –
and that may prompt others to consider
leaving.

- *Respecting.* Many leavers have left reluctantly and
  after much heart-searching. Most have not
  abandoned their faith, but have left because their
  experience of church has damaged their faith or
  inhibited their spiritual development. Many report
  that since leaving they have experienced, alongside
  disorientation and a sense of loss, significant
  spiritual growth – deeper experiences of prayer,
  unexpected freedom in evangelism and greater
  integration of faith and life. We may wonder how
  long this can be sustained in post-Christendom
  without some kind of belonging, but it is vital to
  affirm the integrity of leavers and respect their
  ongoing faith journeys.

- *Resourcing.* Many leavers do not want to return to
  church, but most recognise the need for some kind of
  belonging. This may mean conversations and shared
  meals with other leavers or with friends who are still
  involved in church. 'Post-church' groups are also
  developing, which are similar to churches but are
  usually simpler and have a different ethos from the
  churches leavers have left. Listening to and
  respecting leavers can enable post-Christendom
  churches to offer resources of friendship, hospitality,

---

[27] Jamieson, *Churchless*, 43.

theological reflection and space to explore questions and feelings.[28]

Whatever the reasons for leaving and however these reasons are interpreted, post-Christendom churches can provide open doors for leavers to remain friends, to draw on ecclesial resources and even to return. At the very least, churches might offer an 'exit interview'; some might consider developing a course for leavers (*Omega* rather than *Alpha*?) or a leaving liturgy. Leaving well – knowing that two-way listening has taken place and that relationships are intact – is important for both church and leavers.

Pearse and Matthews concede 'the leavers may be wrong (though it's supremely unlikely that they *all* are)' and recognise that different leavers want different things that may contradict other leavers. But they advocate careful listening.[29] Conversations with leavers and with post-church groups may help churches identify key issues for repentance and renewal. What kinds of churches might leavers rejoin – or not leave in the first place?

- Churches where God is at the centre, rather than the minister, programme or growth targets.
- Churches that nurture authentic friendships rather than insipid 'fellowship' or institutional belonging.
- Churches that are self-critical, alert to destructive interpersonal dynamics and that are working towards healthy community practices.
- Churches that treat adults as adults and encourage spiritual development rather than spoon-feeding their members.

---

[28] See further, Jamieson, *Churchless*, 145–51; Stuart, *So Long*, 125–6.
[29] Pearse and Matthews, *Meeting*, 22.

- Churches that foster dialogue rather than monologue and participation rather than performance.
- Churches that welcome questions, eschew simplistic answers and affirm the dimension of mystery in authentic spirituality.
- Churches that encourage expressions of doubt, anger and lament as well as joyful certainty.
- Churches that are attuned to the pressures of daily life and do not place unrealistic demands on their members.
- Churches that engage creatively and sensitively with contemporary culture and social issues.
- Churches that equip members for the world of work and discipleship beyond the congregation.
- Churches that embrace a holistic understanding of mission and have realistic expectations as marginal communities in post-Christendom.

Through the Front Door

But many people continue to arrive through the front door – enough in some churches for those who leave through the back door to be ignored and their concerns dismissed. Why are people still joining a declining and struggling institution? What attracts them and what obstacles do they encounter? What can we learn from their journeys into church? How can post-Christendom churches welcome more people through the front door, whether believing precedes belonging or belonging precedes believing?

The impact of the Decade of Evangelism on Britain was very limited and the numbers joining the churches through numerous high-profile initiatives were disappointing. Its lasting legacy may be belated acceptance that Christendom models of evangelism are ineffective and alienating within and beyond the churches. Church leaders frequently inveigh against such evangelistic activities and their underlying theology. Many who remain in the churches are also averse to inherited forms of evangelism and, unaware of alternatives, resist further attempts to enlist them in evangelism.

John Finney's research was available early in the decade, but the momentum towards repeating old-style evangelistic strategies was unstoppable. His discoveries about how and why people found faith did at least explain why expensive and massively hyped strategies failed to deliver the promised results. Hopefully, they will preclude further efforts along these lines. They also stimulated or undergirded different evangelistic approaches, which, if not yet fully attuned to post-Christendom realities,[30] are helpful transitional models.

In a moment we will investigate the most popular of these, *Alpha*, but for those unfamiliar with the material it is worth summarising three of Finney's key findings:

- The journey towards faith for many people is a lengthy process, not a sudden crisis, and involves multiple factors.
- The crucial factors are normally personal rather than institutional: friends and family members are more significant than events or activities.
- An awareness of guilt is the precipitating cause of conversion for only a minority of those who have found faith in recent years.

These findings made excellent sense to many Christians, who recognised their own faith journeys and those of friends. But they challenged event-oriented models of evangelism that relied on guilt-focused messages, rationalist

---

[30] See further, Murray: *Post-Christendom*, 225–32.

apologetics and crisis conversions. Laurence Singlehurst offered an alternative approach in his popular *Sowing, Reaping, Keeping*, encouraging churches to adopt more sensitive, patient and realistic strategies.[31]

Robert Warren's investigations midway through the Decade of Evangelism confirmed Finney's findings and added further insights:

- Many come to faith via spirituality rather than doctrine, persuaded by spiritual experience rather than apologetics, searching for identity rather than truth.
- The shift from 'event' to 'process' does not preclude the significance of events within the process or the validity of encouraging, without pressure, 'decision moments'.
- Listening to individuals and their cultural context is crucial if evangelism is to engage with the questions and issues that concern people.

Post-Christendom evangelism should draw gratefully on this research and probe more deeply into the issues it highlights.[32]

Joining the church

For our immediate purposes two things are significant. First, this research suggests post-Christendom churches can expect to encounter *both* 'believing before belonging' and 'belonging before believing'. Friendship with Christians is more likely than invitations to church to stimulate

---

[31] See Laurence Singlehurst, *Sowing, Reaping, Keeping* (London: Crossway, 1995).
[32] See further chapter 5.

believing; but for those journeying towards faith some form of belonging may be crucial. Second, many coming through the front door of the churches are arriving via one of the process evangelism courses that, whether or not their designers engaged with Finney's work, certainly reflect his findings.

Focusing on *Alpha* does not imply whole-hearted endorsement of this course or that similar, though lower profile, courses are less effective.[33] But it has been the busiest path to the front door of the church over the past decade. Our interest in *Alpha* here is less in terms of assessing it as an evangelistic strategy than as a means of unearthing factors that are significant for people joining churches. What features of *Alpha* attract people to the course? Why do some fail to make the transition from *Alpha* to church? What can we learn from those who do and do not join churches?

Four components of *Alpha* seem especially significant by comparison with regular church patterns:

- Friendship – those who participate are generally invited by friends and the course works well if a group gels and friendships develop.
- Food – the intimacy and enjoyment of a shared meal enhances relationships and provides a relaxed and congenial setting for conversation.
- Dialogue – despite lengthy monologue presentations, there is no pressure to respond and there is opportunity for debate, questions and disagreement.

---

[33] Recent research suggests comparable or better results, albeit on a smaller scale: Booker and Ireland, *Evangelism*, 47. For an introduction to the theology and values of *Alpha*, see Nicky Gumbel: *Telling Others: The Alpha Initiative* (Eastbourne: Kingsway, 1994).

- Spiritual experience – the 'Holy Spirit weekend' is the pivot of the course, when apologetics gives way to spiritual encounter.

Some churches with successful *Alpha* courses have struggled to integrate newcomers into regular church life. The transition is often far from smooth. This may be because the course has been bolted on rather than integrated into the church's spirituality, or because the qualities that made *Alpha* attractive to enquirers are less apparent in the church they are invited to join. *Alpha*'s relaxed and friendly ethos has morphed into an institution with multiple meetings and superficial relationships. Instead of opportunities to ask questions and express dissent, there are weekly monologues with no right of reply. The church's home groups are less energising than the course's lively discussions. And where has the food gone? Tea, biscuits and 'a time of fellowship' are poor substitutes for the meals and friendship that made *Alpha* enjoyable. Spiritual encounter is now mediated through performances by 'worship leaders' at which most people are spectators. The more discerning joiners soon realise that many established members are also unsatisfied.

Learning from joiners

Churches respond in various ways to this mismatch. Some decline to make changes, expect newcomers to adjust, and are disappointed by the drop-out rate. Others learn from *Alpha* and allow its practices and ethos to reshape church life. In some places, where churches are unwilling to adapt, new churches are emerging from *Alpha* courses.[34] Remark-

---

[34] Examples are given in *Mission-Shaped Church* (London: Church House, 2004), 155 and Michael Moynagh: *Changing World, Changing Church* (London: Monarch, 2001), 114.

ably, in many places, *Alpha* graduates do join churches despite their dissimilarity from the course through which they found faith. Their enthusiasm and hunger to grow as Christians enables them to overcome obstacles. But is the mismatch between *Alpha* and regular church storing up trouble?

This discussion is not implying *Alpha* is all a church should be, or even that it is an adequate process evangelism course for post-Christendom churches. *Alpha* has its critics,[35] who claim:

- It does not work everywhere and some churches have been disappointed by its impact (and its white, male middle-class ethos).
- Many who do the course are already Christians, using it as a refresher course (which is admirable but inflates the numbers claimed for it).
- It does not start far enough back for post-Christendom and is too modernistic and rationalistic for a postmodern culture.
- Its conservative evangelical and charismatic theology is problematic for many churches (and church leavers).
- Its narrow agenda produces standardised converts rather than disciples who can think for themselves.
- The monologue presentations are unimaginative and over-long and freedom to engage in genuine dialogue is inadequate.
- The 'Holy Spirit' weekend may not be conducive for many who are searching for a less prescriptive

---

[35] See, for example, the sociological analysis in Stephen Hunt, *Anyone for Alpha?* (London: Darton, Longman & Todd, 2001) and the more positive theological appraisal in Booker and Ireland, *Evangelism*, 12–32.

'spiritual encounter'. It moves too quickly from
evangelism to induction, not allowing enough time
for pre-churched people to explore questions of
faith.

Other courses are emerging, such as *Start!* (designed for a
more visually oriented and working-class context) and
Essence (more open-ended and experiential, starting with
spiritual experience).[36] In a plural culture we need many
courses, each of which will pose challenges for the churches
that participants are invited to join. *Alpha* will not, for
instance, appeal to those who prefer to eat at home and
dislike small groups. And as post-Christendom advances,
such invitational approaches may be inadequate.[37]

Alpha has been a phenomenal success in terms of
the numbers it has attracted[38] and numerous encouraging
stories of transformed lives. It may, however, be a transitional approach, pointing us away from ineffective
late-Christendom models of evangelism towards post-
Christendom models yet to emerge. *Alpha* may also indicate a form of church that is attractive to people coming
through the front door. The features that have made *Alpha*
congenial to people considering the Christian faith may be
equally congenial to those who have believed and now want
to belong or those who are not sure what they believe but
want to belong while they explore further. However we
assess the content of *Alpha*, perhaps we can learn most from
its format and ethos.

---

[36] For information, see www.cpas.org.uk. On other courses, see
Booker and Ireland, *Evangelism*, passim.
[37] See Booker and Ireland, *Evangelism*, 66-67.
[38] In 2004 there were 7,000 courses registered in Britain and 1.6
million had already attended a course (6 million worldwide).

Listening at Both Doors

Drawing together the research and listening attentively to joiners and leavers, what can we learn? At first glance we seem to be between a rock and a hard place. *Alpha* may be effective at the front door but for many leavers it represents the pre-packaged theology, privatised spirituality and simplistic approach to mission that impelled them through the back door. Post-church groups may be places of nurture, encouragement and freedom to question which leavers crave as they journey *on* in faith, but they are ineffective with those who are journeying *towards* faith. It is the much-maligned EPC churches with their clear convictions that continue to evangelise the de-churched and semi-churched, and occasionally the pre-churched and anti-churched.

Cannot the same church attract newcomers *and* nurture longstanding members? Must we accept a scenario where churches with open front doors also have open back doors – and where other churches or post-church groups welcome through their front doors only those who have walked through the back doors of other churches? Is *this* our best hope for church after Christendom?

Listening more intently at the back and front doors suggests a more hopeful scenario. We should not expect people at very different stages on the journey to have identical agendas, but there is overlap between aspects of church that attract joiners and aspects of church leavers yearn for. Those who join churches do so because they find in them something worth joining, regardless of whether they yet believe what those churches teach. Those who leave churches do so because they do not find them worth staying in, regardless of whether they still believe most of what they teach.

What are these things that make churches worth joining and staying in? Listening at both doors and cross-referencing what we hear suggests five crucial components:

- Churches that cultivate an earthed spirituality where people encounter God.
- Churches that nurture authentic friendships and healthy community.
- Churches that hold deep convictions but are unfazed by questions and doubts.
- Churches that are open-edged and engage with contemporary culture.
- Churches that stimulate faith development at every stage on the journey.

Presenting these conclusions in various settings has prompted two responses: they are both *attractive* and *achievable*. Developing churches with these characteristics will be challenging, but there is nothing particularly complicated here. To the relief of many, pre-packaged processes and quick-fix methods are neither necessary nor appropriate. This agenda points us to foundational gospel values, which churches from different traditions can affirm and express in diverse ways. Particular components are already well-developed in some churches – the challenge is to combine these components creatively and holistically in churches that are attractive to both joiners and leavers.

Many church leaders respond to this agenda by commenting that this is not just the kind of church that might attract people to join and discourage others from leaving. It is the kind of church to which they themselves want to belong!

Some, however, have concerns about this analysis and proposal. The word 'attractive' raises hackles. First, it sounds suspiciously as if the agenda results from a consumer survey of joiners and leavers. Is this another instance of contemporary consumerism infiltrating and subverting the church? Second, it suggests that the church's primary task is to attract people rather than to incarnate the gospel into post-Christendom society. Is this a reversion to the centripetal, attractional Christendom approach to mission rather than the centrifugal, incarnational approach needed in post-Christendom?

These are important warnings. We need each other's help to detect the persistence of the Christendom mindset and the pervasive influence of consumerism. Learning from those on the margins of our churches is missionally and pastorally responsible, but we must listen critically and reflect theologically on what is said. Where what we hear coheres with core gospel values, we can be confident we are not simply responding to consumer pressure. Where the agenda is congruent with characteristics of the early churches and dissident groups from the Christendom era, we may be rediscovering essential components of post-Christendom churches.

Is it illegitimate to advocate attractive post-Christendom churches? However strongly we affirm the shift from an attractional Christendom stance to an incarnational post-Christendom strategy, incarnational mission does not preclude the need for attractive churches. Attractive churches are the source and outcome of effective incarnational mission.

Others ask if this agenda is 'achievable' within existing churches. Can EPC and other churches embrace the necessary changes (and more radical changes needed to reach pre-churched and anti-churched people for whom *Alpha* is inadequate), or should we build post-Christendom churches on new foundations? Similar questions have often been asked in recent decades. In the 1970s and 1980s the question was: is charismatic renewal sustainable within existing churches or are new churches needed to restore New Testament Christianity? In the 1990s the question was: for effective mission, should we plant new churches or work through existing churches? In chapter 3, we will encounter emerging churches that are questioning the adequacy of inherited churches for post-Christendom.

We have not mentioned Acts 11 in this chapter. At that stage in the story of the early church the only leavers we know about were those who had died (as martyrs or in less honourable circumstances).[39] But Cornelius and his household presented profound challenges as joiners. The hesitant but welcoming response of the Jerusalem church, confirmed and clarified by the Council of Jerusalem, represents the careful listening, theological reflection and cross-referencing with core gospel values commended in this chapter. The result was not only that the front door was opened wide to growing numbers of Gentile converts, but that these unexpected joiners transformed the church.

Our situation in post-Christendom, requiring us to listen to both joiners and leavers, is more complicated than that of the Jerusalem church in Acts 11, but if we are to build faithful and attractive post-Christendom churches we will need what they had – principled flexibility.

---

[39] Acts 5:5–10; 7:54–60.

3

Church After Christendom: Will It Emerge?

Fragmentation and Ecumenism

The disintegration of Christendom made leaving church easier. It also resulted in the fragmentation of Western Christianity as new denominations and smaller networks of churches multiplied. This process began in the sixteenth century as Christendom fractured into competing mini-Christendoms, each with established churches claiming monopolies within emerging European nation-states. It continued throughout the next three centuries as movements of dissent and renewal (Congregationalists, Baptists, Methodists, Brethren, etc.) set up alternative groupings of churches. Some, excluded from existing churches, developed reluctantly; others were eager to establish new churches and denominations.

The proliferation of denominations since the late nineteenth century has saddened or outraged many Christians; others have celebrated their entrepreneurial energy and the recovery of important aspects of the Christian tradition. This fragmentation (exported globally through denominational mission agencies) has continued throughout the final decades of Christendom. Waves of new churches swept through the second half of the twentieth century: examples include intentional Christian communities, Caribbean and other mono-ethnic[1] churches and the House (New) Church movement. Many were evangelical and charismatic; others were nurtured by different theological and spiritual traditions.[2] Further movements have emerged in recent years, stimulating similar mixed reactions.

The ecumenical movement has been an effective counter influence, striving for unity rather than further diversification. But, although this emerged from the Edinburgh World Missionary Conference in 1910, many have queried its interpretation of both unity and mission. The yearning for a united church is rooted in Jesus' prayer in John 17 and the eschatological vision in Revelation 7. There are persuasive theological and missional reasons for pursuing ecclesial unity. But post-Christendom ecumenism will be different from the imposed hierarchical unity of Christendom. It will be organic, missional and messy – but perhaps more effective than twentieth-century efforts to foster unity by consultations, official statements and denominational mergers.

Church planting in the 1990s can be understood as an expression of post-Christendom ecumenism. Many suspected this movement would catalyse further fragmentation, but it mainly planted new churches within existing denominations and exhibited unusual interdenominational cooperation.[3] Attempts to plant officially ecumenical churches were fraught with difficulties, stymied by out-

---

[1] Less than ideal terminology, but preferable to 'ethnic' or 'ethnic minority'.

[2] See, for instance, John J. Vincent, *Alternative Church* (Belfast: Christian Journals, 1976), Jeanne Hinton, *Communities: Stories of Christian Communities in Europe* (Guildford: Eagle, 1993), Peter Hocken, *Streams of Renewal* (Carlisle: Paternoster, 1997) and Andrew Walker, *Restoring the Kingdom: The Radical Christianity of the House Church Movement* (Guildford: Eagle, 1998).

[3] Although it primarily involved evangelicals.

moded bureaucratic and institutional Christendom-style ecumenism. Since 2000, however, ecumenical church planting has displayed a lighter touch and greater flexibility – hopeful signs of lessons learned and a more organic approach.

But if some feared that church planting might be ecumenically disruptive, others suspected that many newly planted churches were simply clones of existing churches, inadequately attuned to a changing cultural context. It was evident by the mid–1990s that unrealistic numerical targets suggested in the fevered atmosphere of a church planting consultation (though never officially adopted by denominations) would not be achieved. This, coupled with concerns about the viability and health of newly planted churches and looming leadership shortages, prompted a slowdown in church planting. A necessary pause for reflection allowed discussion of missiological and ecclesiological issues sidelined in the frenetic activity of the first half of the decade. Were the new churches missional or effective? Were we planting churches that could incarnate the gospel into the many subcultures of postmodern, post-Christendom society?

This pause drastically reduced the numbers of churches that most denominations and networks planted during the second half of the 1990s. Only quite recently has evidence emerged of a new wave of church planting, which will hopefully be contextually more sensitive and missionally more focused.[4]

But already in the late 1990s another wave of new churches was emerging. This overlapped with the church planting movement, in terms of personnel and motivation, but there were major differences. This was an apparently spontaneous phenomenon. Churches were emerging in various places without central planning, coordination or

---

[4] See further George Lings and Stuart Murray, *Church Planting: Past, Present and Future* (Cambridge: Grove, 2003).

consultation. Loose networking, shared stories, 'blogging' on websites and developing friendships were all that connected otherwise isolated initiatives. It was similar to the early years of the House Church movement (except the blogging!) before this became more organised and reverted to traditional ecclesiology.

Unlike the House Churches and the church planting movement, the churches that have emerged in the past few years have been remarkably diverse. Many do not regard themselves as church plants; indeed, they distrust the terminology and agenda of church planting. But some of what is emerging can be interpreted as responses to missiological and ecclesiological questions which the church planting movement belatedly raised.[5] Emerging churches are incarnating the gospel into parts of society that traditional forms of church planting did not touch.

Is this the latest and most chaotic manifestation of the fragmentation of Christendom? Is it a further threat to ecumenism? Or is this a harbinger of missional and ecclesial renewal in the Western church? This chapter addresses the questions raised at the end of chapter 2. Are new churches needed for post-Christendom or can churches from the Christendom era reinvent themselves for this strange new world? Will church after Christendom *evolve* or *emerge*? And if it emerges, are we witnessing the start of the emergence of church after Christendom?

Emerging Churches

Some emerging churches resonate with issues discussed in the previous two chapters. Most endorse and practise

---

[5] This interpretation is offered in *Mission-shaped Church* (London: Church House, 2004).

belonging before believing. Many advocate centred-set ecclesiology, although they do not always fully understand it. And church leavers' concerns inform the priorities and shape the ethos of emerging churches, within which they are well represented. These developments have raised hopes that something significant is afoot which might recalibrate the church for post-Christendom.[6]

St Peter's is a 140-foot barge with a capacity of 100 moored in West India Dock, near Canary Wharf in East London's Dock-lands. Its parish is not the local neighbourhood but the thousands who work in Canary Wharf. St Peter's offers Wednesday lunchtime teaching events, prayer for forty-five minutes at 7.45 on Tuesday mornings and a Thursday lunchtime discipleship course.

I-church is a diocesan web-based church. 'Visitors are welcome to *I-church* in the same way that they are to any physical church. They can read the posts, and are welcome to any of the meetings or events … One of the key purposes of *I-church* is to provide a community for those who do not find participant membership of a local church easy, and it will therefore reflect an inclusive attitude to Christian faith and discipleship.'[7]

The team wondered what the church they were planting would be called. They had decided to wait until local people named it. Naming implied ownership and they wanted the church to be indigenous rather than imposed. In fact, they did not even use

---

[6] What follows (here and in the first part of chapter 4) reworks material presented in Stuart Murray, *Changing Mission: Learning from the Newer Churches* (London: CTBI, 2005), which gives numerous further examples of emerging churches and additional sources of information. See also Murray, *Post-Christendom*, 253–8; George Lings, *Encounters on the Edge* (Sheffield: The Sheffield Centre, quarterly) and www.emergingchurch.info.

[7] See www.i-church.org.

'church' to describe what was emerging. Eventually local people said the church needed a name – and were surprised to hear this was up to them. The name they chose was simple, geographical and resonated with the community's history. It was not a name the planting team had considered!

She had not belonged to any church for several years, having left her church at a time of personal pain and struggle. But she had welcomed the invitation to participate in a table church and had taken part actively in all that happened. She seemed to feel at home, but we were uncertain until she told us over the washing up (a vital aspect of table church) that she was usually 'allergic' to Christians but had really enjoyed the evening.

Vaux started in 1998, basically in response to being bored in church! Sitting in pews, singing 'light-rock' songs, listening to long orations … didn't fit with who we felt we were as people … rather than give up on the whole thing, which we saw so many doing, we decided to try to do something about it. *Vaux* is essentially about worship. We have come to see that to worship with integrity you have to give something of yourself – something that has integrity for you as a person or community. So the only reason we have great video and graphics stuff is because there are people who are into that … similarly with the dance, theatre, liturgy, installations, readings, music and food that have sometimes formed part of services.'[8]

The Baptist Times reported on 'the church with choice', a community church offering nine 'zones' in its morning service (prayer, teaching, counselling, discussion, praise, quiet, fellowship, children and teenagers). After café-style refreshments, everyone disperses into the zones, free to move between them until everyone gathers again for prayer, praise and communion.[9]

---

[8] See further www.vaux.net.
[9] *The Baptist Times*, 27 May, 2004, 2.

Emerging churches are so disparate there are exceptions to any generalisations. Most are too new and too fluid to classify, let alone assess their significance. There is no consensus yet about what language to use: 'new ways of being church'; 'emerging church'; 'fresh expressions of church'; 'future church'; 'church next'; or 'the coming church'. The terminology used here contrasts 'inherited' and 'emerging' churches.

Nor is there any agreed scheme for categorising what is emerging. There are trends and patterns, shared values and common features, but emerging churches espouse diverse convictions, are motivated by different concerns and assess their development by varying criteria. One scheme utilises categories suggested in chapter 1: different emerging churches are shaped by interaction with the semi-churched, de-churched, pre-churched, post-churched or anti-churched. Another (used in this chapter) builds on the proposal that three essential aspects of church are mission, community and worship, and categorises emerging churches according to their primary motivation.[10]

And the significance of these developments is hotly debated. Some invest great hope in emerging churches, regarding them as signs of renewal, evidence of missional engagement with a changing culture, harbingers of church growth in Western society beyond unrelenting decline. Others are sceptical, even scathing. They suspect we have been this way before, are convinced there is (ecclesially as elsewhere) nothing new under the sun, and are concerned this is another distraction from genuine missional engagement

---

[10] See Robert Warren, *Being Human, Being Church: Spirituality and Mission in the Local Church* (London: Marshall Pickering, 1995) and the adaptation of his model to emerging churches in Stuart Murray and Anne Wilkinson-Hayes, *Hope from the Margins* (Cambridge: Grove, 2000), 17.

with a culture that has proved remarkably impervious to previous ecclesial reconfiguration.

What follows does not prejudge the significance of emerging churches but surveys the landscape, highlighting features relevant to all churches after Christendom. Emerging churches may not have all the answers, but they are raising many crucial questions.

Mission-oriented Emerging Churches

For some observers, mission is the non-negotiable starting point. They are reluctant to describe non-missional groups as 'emerging church' and suspect some emerging churches are self-indulgent distractions from the mission to which post-Christendom churches are called. Internal reconfiguration that does not impact the world beyond the church does not impress them. They are interested only in churches emerging from missional reflection on and engagement with contemporary culture.

Many emerging churches represent responses to diverse mission contexts. Some are attempts to establish culturally specific churches in particular places or sectors of society from which churches have been absent. Some began as creative approaches to community engagement. They were not intended to become churches but developed into churches as those involved found their ecclesiology transformed by engagement with the community they were serving. Some emerged from evangelistic initiatives, which were originally perceived as conduits through which members might be added to existing churches. They grew into churches as those involved found the culture gap between new Christians and church too wide.

Inherited church developed when 'churchgoing' was normal and most families had some connection with churches (although this was less typical in urban communities). Mission, always peripheral to institutional maintenance, meant support for overseas missionaries, efforts to galvanise the faith of 'latent Christians' who comprised the bulk of the population and attempts to improve society and care for needy individuals. Evangelicals and liberals debated the priority attached to different aspects of mission, but there was widespread agreement that mission was something churches 'did', alongside other activities.

In post-Christendom, mission is a mindset before it is activities, and 'latent Christian' is an unhelpful concept. Churches are alien institutions telling a story few know or understand. Some emerging churches are grappling with the paradigm shift involved in becoming truly missional.

Restructuring churches for mission

Some churches have wisely resisted the temptation to weld mission activities onto an essentially maintenance-oriented institution, recognising this paradigm shift requires wholesale ecclesial restructuring.

- *Seeker-oriented church* restructures church around the needs of 'seekers' – those who may become joiners. Thorough community research informs the style and content of 'seeker services', performances through which enquirers can encounter Christianity without participating. 'Belonging before believing' allows anonymous attendance. Converts join midweek believers' services.[11]

---

[11] See Lee Strobel, *Inside the Mind of Unchurched Harry and Mary: How to Reach Friends and Family Who Avoid God and the Church* (Grand Rapids: Zondervan, 1993) and Bill and Lynne Hybels, *Rediscovering Church* (Grand Rapids: Zondervan,

- *Purpose-driven church* restructures church around five ecclesial purposes: worship, evangelism, fellowship, discipleship and ministry. A comprehensive strategy is designed to draw people into church and encourage them to grow as disciples. Decisions about staff, programmes, activities and finance are related explicitly to the core purposes. The church's mission is understood in relation to five concentric circles: the community, the crowd, the congregation, the committed and the core.[12]

- *Cell church* operates as a network of small neighbourhood churches that meet weekly as cells and join together for corporate celebrations. Cells engage in relational evangelism, expecting to grow and divide. Core values include the centrality of Jesus; the expectation that members will participate and mature; the development of honest, loving community; and growth by multiplication. In some models, the cell is primary; in others cell and celebration have equal weight. But the cell *is* church, not a peripheral or secondary group, and does everything inherited churches do.[13]

---

[11] (*continued*) 1997). For details of this model in a British context, read Martin Robinson, *A World Apart: Creating a Church for the Unchurched - Learning from Willow Creek* (Crowborough: Monarch, 1992) or see www.willowcreek.org.uk or www.run.org.uk.

[12] For further details, see www.purposedriven.com or Rick Warren, *The Purpose-driven Church* (Grand Rapids: Zondervan, 1995). For a British perspective, see David Beer, *Releasing your Church to Grow* (Eastbourne: Kingsway, 2004).

[13] For further details of cell churches in Britain, see www.celluk.co.uk or read Laurence Singlehurst, *Loving the Lost* (Eastbourne: Kingsway, 2001).

- *G12 cell church* shares many assumptions and values
  of cell church, but there are significant differences in
  structure and ethos. The model develops through
  establishing groups of twelve, each of whom forms
  their own further group of twelve. Cells are
  homogeneous, with groups for men, women, young
  people and children. G12 means 'government of
  twelve': the model is hierarchical but affirms the
  leadership potential of every Christian.[14]
- *Minsters* (reworking models from early English
  Christianity) are large churches with multiple staff,
  skills and resources that can be resource churches
  with missional responsibility for larger areas –
  centres of support, training and strategic
  coordination for surrounding smaller churches.
  Some advocate minsters as an alternative to efforts
  to maintain a parish system stretched to breaking
  point.[15]
- *Clusters* are more flexible and mission-focused than
  congregations, but larger and less homogeneous than
  cells. They are congregation-sized communities that
  do not carry the weight of being fully fledged
  churches. They have a clear missional identity,
  around which their members gather; but the
  involvement of these members in celebrations and
  cells offers a broader church experience and greater
  intimacy.[16]
- *Café-style church* represents restructuring of a more
  practical kind. It involves churches setting out their

---

[14] See further www.g12harvest.org and Colin Dye, *Hearts on Fire*
(London: Dovewell, 2002).

[15] See Nick Spencer, *Parochial Vision: The Future of the English
Parish* (Carlisle: Paternoster, 2004).

[16] For example, see www.sttoms.net.

normal meeting place in café format, with groups of
chairs around small tables. Most café-style churches
have a similar philosophy to seeker-oriented
churches. Their format may be interactive or
presentational, but they hope the atmosphere is
welcoming.[17]

Participants in other emerging churches may regard these
models with disdain as still rooted in the ethos of inherited
church and part of the problem! Others will recognise similar core values to their own emerging church. However we
assess them, they are attempts to reconfigure church for
mission. This passion would not go amiss in some apparently more edgy but missionally deficient emerging
churches.

But relying on a centripetal model that expects 'seekers'
to attend services in church buildings is inadequate. In
post-Christendom, where interest in spirituality does not
readily translate into churchgoing, a centrifugal approach is
necessary. Belonging may precede believing, but we must go
to people instead of hoping they will come to us.

Importing church into new places

Some emerging churches are responding to this challenge by
importing church into places that in post-Christendom are
culturally more congenial than church buildings. This is not
entirely new: church planters have used community centres,
snooker halls, schools, shops and other venues. But these
locations did not shape the churches they planted, except
superficially. Church planters in the 1990s took church

---

[17] For examples, see Graham Horsley, *Planting New Churches:
Conference Report and Study Guide* (London: The Methodist
Church, 2001), 24-29 and www.regenthall.co.uk/cafechurch/.

geographically closer to people; some emerging churches are taking church *culturally* closer.

- *Workplace church*: some find relationships with Christian colleagues more authentic and sustaining than their experience of neighbourhood church. They regard workplace church as their main Christian community. Some workplace churches emerge spontaneously; others are established deliberately to respond to the demands of contemporary work patterns and opportunities for faith-sharing with friends at work.[18]
- *Pub church*: several forms of pub church have emerged. Some hire a room and hold services similar to those held in church buildings. Others organise special events to entertain and challenge those who participate. Others are integrated into the pub community and run open events which regulars accept as part of pub life.[19]
- *Club-culture church*: some people feel greater affinity with those who share their love of dance, music and clubbing than those they work with or live near. Some club-culture churches operate in city-centre clubs, pubs and wine bars. Their members participate in the clubs, building relationships and inviting friends to church activities. Others have developed their own venues to host culturally appropriate events.[20]

[18] See Moynagh, *Changing World*, 71–5.
[19] For examples, see www.zacsplace.org, www.pubchurch.com, and www.pubchurch.co.uk.
[20] For examples, see www.qpcrypt.com and Jeanne Hinton, *Changing Churches* (London: CTBI, 2002), 69–71.

- *Café church* (rather than café-style church) means Christians meeting in a café with people for whom this is a natural meeting-place. The focus may be post-churched or pre-churched people; there is often an emphasis on the arts and alternative worship; and Christians may or may not run the café.[21]
- *Enterprise church* involves building relationships through shared projects and enterprises. These relationships are the context, not only for faith-sharing, but for the emergence of indigenous faith communities, rooted in the local culture rather than imposed from outside.[22]
- *Cyber-church*: if pubs, clubs and workplaces are centres of community, so is the Internet. Various groups are forming web-based congregations, with or without physical meetings. Some use the Internet to build and sustain church communities but encourage members also to meet together. Others dispense entirely with physical community and connect only through the Internet.[23]

These are examples of contexts into which Christians are importing church. They are evidence of missional creativity but raise many questions, especially about the nature of Christian community, their sustainability and connections to other expressions of church.

---

[21] For examples, see www.cafechurch.org and www.cafechurch.org.au.

[22] See Michael Frost and Alan Hirsch, *The Shaping of Things to Come: Innovation and Mission for the 21st Century Church* (Peabody: Hendrickson, 2004), 24–5.

[23] British examples include:
   www.webchurch.org (Church of Scotland);
   www.i-church.org (Oxford diocese) and
   www.church.co.uk (Oasis Trust).

Incarnating church into different cultures

Importing church into different places may also involve changes in style and ethos in order to develop culturally attuned as well as appropriately located churches. Being culturally attuned is a feature of other emerging churches trying to incarnate the gospel into the many subcultures of post-Christendom. These emerging churches have concluded that it is as unrealistic to expect inherited churches to embrace multiple subcultures as it is to expect people who are culturally distant from those churches to leap this gap. An alternative approach is to start churches within these networks and subcultures.

- *Network church*, alert to the networked nature of contemporary society, incarnates the gospel and church into various networks, rather than expecting people to join churches in neighbourhoods where they do little but sleep. What members have in common is not where they live but who they know and why. Their constituency is defined demographically, not geographically.[24]
- *Culture-specific church*: some ask what church might look like if it emerges in diverse subcultures and develops in culturally specific forms. The aim is to catalyse indigenous churches in communities beyond the reach of inherited churches. Churches are emerging, for instance, in Goth, sci-fi, rave, techno and other underground music subcultures.[25]

---

[24] For examples, see *Mission-shaped*, 8, 62–4.
[25] See, for example, the story, beliefs and values of a church rooted in the London underground music scene: www.gloriousundead.com.

- *Youth church* incarnates the gospel in ecclesial forms appropriate for young people. This may be neighbourhood- or network-based, although typically relationships develop along network lines. It may operate through regional celebrations or weekly congregations and often has a cell-based pastoral system. It is also about empowerment – emerging churches which young people themselves shape and lead.[26]
- *Young adult church*. What happens when people reach the upper age limit of youth churches – does the age limit stretch? If it does not stretch, do they join inherited churches? An alternative option is emerging young adult church.[27]
- *Children's church*: some have designed churches for children, rather than trying to integrate them into churches designed primarily for adults. Most are churches adults lead, but some empower children to help shape church. The most impressive examples involve adults not only running events but visiting *every child* in their home *every week*.[28]
- *Church for marginalised groups*: churches for deaf people, homeless people, recovering drug abusers or alcoholics, ex-offenders, paedophiles, New Age travellers, people with mental health problems. In a fragmented society, we may need churches

---

[26] See John Hall, 'The Rise of the Youth Congregation and its Missiological Significance' (PhD thesis: University of Birmingham, 2003) and Graham Cray, *Youth Congregations and the Emerging Church* (Cambridge: Grove, 2002).

[27] For a leading example, see www.churchnext.net – the website of *Tribal Generation*.

[28] For one model of children's church, see Geoff Pearson and Philip Clark, *Kids Klubs* (Cambridge: Grove, 2001).

specialising in responding to marginalised
communities.

- *Indigenous neighbourhood churches*. Reshaping
churches for mission means starting with the mission
context: missiology precedes ecclesiology. Authentic
churches emerge from interaction between the gospel
and different contexts. This is a core value of a new
wave of emerging urban churches.[29]

Some of these emerging churches raise the spectre of 'homogeneous units' associated with 1980s church growth
ideology. On the basis of research indicating that people
preferred to join churches comprising their own kind of
people, strategists advocated evangelism within homogeneous units, which if effective often created homogeneous
churches. Such churches may be conducive to members of a
particular network or subculture, but are they healthy envi-
ronments in which disciples can mature through interaction
with those who are different?

Critics in inherited churches, however, need both to
assess the homogeneity in their own churches and to
develop viable alternative strategies to incarnate the gospel
in under-represented subcultures. Are one-size-fits-all
churches sustainable in post-Christendom? If not, how can
diversified post-Christendom churches interact, learn
together and express the oneness for which Jesus prayed?

Community-oriented Emerging Churches

Some churches have reconfigured their own community life
as they have listened to the wider community, discerned its

---

[29] For examples, see www.unoh.org and
www.urbanexpression.org.uk.

rhythms, made friends and developed partnerships to respond to particular needs. Through their participation they have recognised the cultural chasm between church and community and have searched for new forms of church in their context.

Churches shaped by community engagement

- *Midweek church*. For many who participate only in midweek church activities (parents and toddlers, senior citizens' lunches, etc.), attendance on Sundays is inconvenient or culturally alien. Instead of persisting with the vain hope some will eventually make this transition, midweek church adds new elements to midweek activities and creates church around existing groups.[30]
- *Project church*. Churches participating in community projects, as initiators or partners with other agencies, have been deeply affected by their experiences. Churches are emerging from community projects, accidentally or by design. Some Christians effectively view community engagement as an alternative to participation in inherited church.[31]
- *7-day-a-week church*. Some churches have initiated projects that are so all-embracing it is difficult to know where church stops and project begins. They challenge the assumption that church consists essentially in worship services and other traditional ecclesial activities, alongside which community projects run. They suggest church is fluid and multifaceted.[32]

---

[30] See *Mission-Shaped Church*, 61 and Booker and Ireland, *Evangelism*, 166–8.

[31] See Murray and Wilkinson-Hayes, *Hope*, 7–9.

[32] See Hinton, *Changing Churches*, 62–3.

- *Post-Alpha church*. The difficulty noted in chapter 2
  – the mismatch between the community ethos of the
  Alpha course and that of some churches that run
  Alpha – has resulted in the emergence of new
  churches formed from people who have taken the
  course.[33]

These developments are encouraging signs that community
engagement has impacted the churches as well as the
communities. Such mutuality (like the double conversion of
Peter and Cornelius in Acts 11) is healthy. But in
post-Christendom, how long can churches sustain community activities without recruiting new members?

Churches shaped by community dynamics

Other churches are emerging because forms of community
in inherited church neither attract potential joiners nor
sustain existing members. Those who join through *Alpha*
struggle with the community dynamics of inherited
churches. And many church leavers grieve the lack of
authentic community and yearn for something deeper and
more rounded. Churches in this section are expressions of
the recovery of small-scale church emerging across Western
culture.[34]

- *Table church* is not simply church meeting in homes
  after a shared meal. Wary of the demise of laughter

---

[33] Examples are given in *Mission-shaped Church*, 155 and
Moynagh, *Changing*, 114.
[34] See Robert and Julia Banks, *The Church Comes Home: Building Community and Mission in Church Homes* (Peabody:
Hendrickson, 1998) and Wolfgang Simson, *Houses that Change
the World: The Return of the House Churches* (Carlisle: OM Publishing, 1998).

and conversation, formality and stilted religiosity
that can result from moving from dining room to
lounge, table churches meet around the table. Several
use 'table liturgies' that interweave many elements,
combining formal structure and informal setting.

- *Household church* is a term used by some who want
  to retain small-scale church despite growing
  numbers. Their strategy is to limit the community to
  the size of a household and multiply rather than
  expand households. Household churches are more
  flexible than cell churches.[35]

- *Base ecclesial communities* emerged in the late 1960s
  in poor communities in Latin America, resourced by
  liberation theologians, as responses to a shortage of
  priests and a context of oppression. These very local
  communities study the Bible and pray together but
  also engage in social and economic action. A few
  examples have emerged in Britain.[36]

- *Small Christian communities* have similarities in
  ethos and structure to base ecclesial communities
  and represent an indigenous version of these,
  fostered especially by the *New Way of Being Church*
  network.[37]

- *Organic church*: for some Christians, even
  small-scale church feels organised rather than
  organic. Some have embarked on journeys
  towards simpler forms of church, gradually
  dismantling institutional aspects of church in the

---

[35] For example, see www.thecrowdedhouse.org/homesweet. htm.

[36] For examples, see www.emergingchurch.info/stories/
basecommunities/index.htm and www.stmargaretmarys.org.uk
/bec1.html.

[37] See Jeanne Hinton and Peter Price, *Changing Communities:
Creating Church from the Grassroots* (London: CTBI, 2003).

hope of finding authentic and unencumbered community.[38]

- *Post-church communities* (mentioned in chapter 2) are gatherings for church leavers who do not want to remain isolated and welcome opportunities to meet with others on similar journeys.[39]

Churches emerging from discontent with the quality of community in inherited church can be inward-looking rather than missional. But renewing the community dimension of church may be a crucial prerequisite for effective and sustainable mission. Small-scale churches offer intimate community and are attractive to many. But are they too small and fragile to be sustainable and missionally effective? Can one encounter the transcendence as well as the immanence of God around the dining table? Are small-scale churches threatening to those who want to explore Christianity in a less intense environment?

Worship-oriented Emerging Churches

Turmoil over worship styles, unsurprising in light of changes and fragmentation in contemporary culture, has prompted the development of another group of emerging churches. Content with neither inherited forms of worship nor the charismatic and informal approach of many churches since the 1970s, they are exploring alternatives.

Alternative worship

Alt.worship (as alternative worship is often known) has been defined as 'liturgical innovation characterised by

---

[38] For example, see www.organicchurch.org.uk.
[39] See Jamieson, *Churchless Faith* and *Journeying.*

communal participation, employment of popular cultural resources, a rediscovery of ancient liturgy and an apprecia- tion of creativity and the arts'.[40] It has been interpreted as an attempt to recombine three essential elements of worship: mystery, hospitality and participation.

Alt.worship is a distinct expression of emerging church, though aspects of alt.worship are influential in other emerg- ing churches and some inherited churches. Characteristic features include an emphasis on space, environment, ambi- ence and context; creative use of diverse technologies, multimedia, the arts and symbolism; a multidirectional, individualised and decentred approach; eclectic use of litur- gical resources; an open-ended experience, allowing multiple interpretations; a participative ethos; and a con- templative mood.[41]

Those who plan and host alt.worship events value an understanding of mission that transcends evangelism; an approach to faith that encourages questions, mystery and journeying; an environment where issues of theology, social justice and ethics can be discussed freely and non- judgementally; a non-dogmatic, hospitable and gender- inclusive community; and support for engagement with environmental and global issues. At its best, alt.worship represents a serious attempt to develop a holistic and earthed spirituality. It has attracted especially post- evangelical and post-charismatic church leavers.

Whether alt.worship represents a viable way forward for post-Christendom churches may depend on its capacity to transcend features some discern in alt.worship circles, including uncritical adoption of postmodern cultural

---

[40] Steve Taylor, 'A New Way of Being Church' (PhD thesis: Uni- versity of Otago, 2003), 2.

[41] Among many websites, see especially www.alternativeworship.org and www.smallfire.org.

values; introspection, angst and reactivity in groups formed from those disillusioned by other churches; individualism and self-centredness in multidirectional worship and generally homogenous groups; and introversion, given the aversion to evangelism in some communities.

Culture-specific worship

Alt.worship is not the only expression of emerging church energised by re-imagining worship.

- *Mono-ethnic church*. By far the largest expression of emerging church is the burgeoning mono-ethnic churches fast becoming the predominant form of church in many inner-city areas. Some resist designating these as emerging churches: their ecclesiology is often traditional and their ethos quite different from other emerging churches. Their inclusion here reminds both inherited and emerging churches that white Christians alone will not effectively incarnate the gospel in multicultural Britain. A primary factor in their emergence (apart from racism and inhospitality in inherited churches) is the desire to worship using their heart language and a style that enables participants to encounter God within their own culture.
- *Contextual liturgy* earths worship in the thought-forms, language, ethos and rhythms of the local community. This does not mean abandoning inherited forms of worship that have sustained generations of Christians and continue symbolically to unite the global church. But it means recognising the influence of Christendom which standardised, and exported as normative, what began as local and contextual forms of worship.

These expressions of church raise again questions about homogeneity and the need to develop post-Christendom churches that are contextual and open, that find a balance between the global and the local.

Customised worship

Another approach that affirms diversity but avoids division is the development of customised worship. Some churches recognise the legitimacy of different cultural expressions but resist homogeneous groups and fragmentation. They have encouraged various forms of worship within their existing ecclesial framework.

- *Multi-congregational church* operates through several congregations, usually on the same premises. Each has a distinctive worship style, mission focus and community expression. This model offers an alternative to the proliferation of culture-specific churches. It facilitates cross-fertilising and growth in maturity through links with people who are different.[42]

- *Menu church*. Resisting division into separate congregations, but recognising the value of diverse expressions of worship, teaching and community, menu church provides different forms of church within a single ecclesial framework. Church members participate in these without losing their identity as members of one community, or choose various activities before a concluding united act of worship.[43]

---

[42] See, for example, *Encounters on the Edge* 8 (Sheffield: Church Army, 2000).

[43] For an example, see *The Baptist Times*, 27 May, 2004, 2.

- *Multicultural church*. There are numerous
  multi-ethnic churches in Britain – some with multiple
  ethnic groups represented, others with two or three
  main groups. Many are working hard to be
  multicultural. Some include members of various
  ethnic groups in all aspects of church; some learn
  songs in several languages; some are grappling with
  issues of power and control.

For theological and missiological reasons, some argue,
churches in a multi-ethnic society should not endorse or
enhance existing divisions. But multiculturalism is a
disputed concept in Western society. Developing multicultural church is an ongoing challenge for inherited and
emerging churches, whatever the commitment in principle
to inclusivity and heterogeneity.

New monasticism

Re-imagining worship cannot be restricted to what happens
when Christians meet together. It involves fresh thinking
about daily spirituality and rhythms of living. For some this
means drawing on ancient liturgical traditions or embracing a rule of life similar to that in monastic communities. As
with alt.worship, this does not mean reviving ancient forms
of inherited church, but remixing old and new elements.
Some discern a new monasticism emerging.

- *Dispersed church*: some are committed to dispersed
  church, a community with shared values and a rule
  of life. Participating regularly – alone or with others
  – in a daily office sustains them and binds them to
  this community. Involvement in dispersed church
  does not preclude participation in 'gathered' church,

but for some dispersed church is their primary
community.[44]

- *Common-purse communities* also have a rule of life
  and daily rhythms of worship, but members live
  together and share possessions and resources. For
  many of these Anabaptism – which some interpret as
  a radical monastic movement – has been an
  inspiration and resource.[45]

- *New monastic orders* are emerging, usually focused
  on mission. They too have rules of life (adapted from
  traditional monastic vows) and patterns of daily
  prayer.[46]

- *Boiler rooms* have emerged from the 24–7 youth
  prayer movement. Alongside prayer groups in
  diverse locations, 'boiler rooms' have emerged,
  'houses of prayer, mission, art and pilgrimage
  modelled on the ancient Celtic Christian
  communities and sometimes described as
  "millennium 3 monasteries"'.[47]

These examples of new monasticism are instances of emerging church that transcend our categories of mission,
community and worship. They span the inherited/emerging
church divide as new expressions of ancient forms of
church. Whether they will thrive and proliferate or be
short-lived experiments will be unclear for some time, but
they may offer ways of sustaining spirituality, inspiring
counter-cultural discipleship and enabling creative mission
in post-Christendom.

---

[44] See, for example, www.northumbriacommunity.org.
[45] See, for example, www.bruderhof.co.uk and www.jesus.
org.uk.
[46] See, for example, www.jacobswell.org.uk and
www.sttoms.net.
[47] See www.24-7prayer.com.

What is Emerging?

Perhaps the most evocative image for describing and inter-preting emerging church is a child's toy, the kaleidoscope. Each time the viewer looks through the spy hole at the brightly coloured shards they have reconfigured them-selves; different patterns have appeared. The basic elements are unchanged, but there are many ways of displaying them. In emerging churches foundational aspects of church – mission, worship and community – reappear as ancient and contemporary elements combine in intriguing new ways.

It is premature to try to assess the significance of emerg-ing church. What is emerging is young, fluid, diverse, provisional and still developing. We cannot know for some time what this widespread but uncoordinated phenomenon presages.

The significance of emerging churches is not numerical. They have generated huge interest, but the numbers involved are limited. Stories are often recycled, giving an unwarranted impression of proliferation. Some disappear as quickly as they appear. Some struggle on, making little impact beyond their core group. Some much-lauded models have very limited appeal. Some pioneer radical initiatives before reverting to inherited patterns. Some implode beneath the weight of internal or external expectations.

But we should not underestimate the significance of emerging churches. Many began recently and are small by design; their proliferation may hardly have begun. Emerging churches have developed spontaneously and rap-idly. Although informal story-sharing and networking has prompted further initiatives, there has been little coordina-tion or organisation. This phenomenon is not dissimilar to significant renewal movements in church history. And, as Walter Brueggemann reminds us, there is biblical justifica-tion for watching the margins: 'Our theological tradition has a peculiar congeniality with these shrill voices at the margin because the biblical story is a tradition of marginality that begins in the slave labour camps of Egypt or among Canaanite peasants and culminates in the cross.'[48]

Surveying the scene as we have done might convey the impression that any changes are superficial and stylistic. This is sometimes the case, but emerging church involves more than this. Beneath the surface are sophisticated cultural debate, missiological engagement and increasing theological reflection. Despite their diversity, emerging churches evince similar theological emphases: creativity rooted in God as Creator; community rooted in God as Trinity; and contextualisation rooted in God incarnate in Jesus.

Inherited churches sometimes express concern about heterodox theology in emerging churches – especially those without theologically trained leaders or accountability to inherited church representatives. Emerging churches, and their advocates, sometimes respond by emphasising their orthodoxy. They may be culturally creative, but they do not want to appear theologically innovative. This is understandable but disappointing. There are encouraging exceptions, but many emerging churches are unadventurous in theology. Some remarkably innovative models on the cutting edge of contemporary culture seem unwilling to extend their ecclesiological creativity to other aspects of theology. Theological timidity may be more dangerous than heterodoxy to emerging churches. Ecclesiological renewal and missiological initiative needs undergirding with theological reflection.

Emerging churches *may* be self-indulgent, introverted experiments catering primarily for bored middle-class

---

[48] Walter Brueggemann, *Interpretation and Obedience: From Faithful Reading to Faithful Living* (Minneapolis: Fortress, 1991), 199.

churchgoers unsatisfied with naïve theology and banal liturgy. Some may be last-ditch attempts to breathe fresh life into dying models. Others may be angst-ridden communities of like-minded dissidents united by discontent. Others again may be tentative forays into unfamiliar territory from which pioneers will return licking their wounds.

On the other hand, emerging churches *may* be forerunners of a missional movement that will negotiate the transition into post-Christendom. They may herald an ecclesial revolution as far-reaching in its effects as the fourth-century Christendom shift but which brings Christendom to an end. They may catalyse renewal in church and society across Western culture. They may kick-start recovery from decades of decline and incarnate the gospel effectively into communities where it is virtually absent.

Different forms of emerging church may, of course, be interpreted differently. Some may be misguided experiments that mercifully disappear before doing much damage. Some may be transitional models pointing the way forward to expressions of church that will thrive in post-Christendom. Some may be creative initiatives that (like some previous movements) fade after injecting fresh ways of thinking and new resources into inherited churches. But some may be forerunners of church after Christendom.

Examining the models in this chapter through the post-Christendom lens, several raise issues, by design or default, which post-Christendom churches will need to address:[49]

- Purpose-driven church: post-Christendom churches will be unable to sustain the multifaceted activities of the past and must focus on core purposes.

---

[49] See also Murray, *Post-Christendom*, 259–60.

- Seeker-sensitive church: post-Christendom churches must be sensitive to visitors who are unfamiliar with church culture, but in post-Christendom it will not be visitors but missional churches who are the 'seekers'.
- Cell church: purged of hierarchical tendencies and unrealistic expectations, this is a sustainable model for marginal churches in an alien environment.
- Minsters and clusters: given the imminent demise of the Christendom parish model, these are creative ways of reconfiguring and maximising the limited resources available to post-Christendom churches.
- Café-style church: as churches discovered in the fourth century as they moved into huge buildings, architecture and seating are influential. Lecture halls and front-focused performance venues may be inappropriate for post-Christendom churches.
- Importing church into new places: an attractional approach that assumes church buildings are congenial for mission must be replaced by an approach that infiltrates society and incarnates the gospel in many venues.
- Culture-specific church: inherited churches marginalise many contemporary subcultures, but cultural attunement must be balanced by counter-cultural witness. Reconciliation and inclusivity are essential gospel reflexes.
- Youth church: these and other age-specific churches may be necessary, but effective inter-generational processes are also crucial for pilgrim churches in post-Christendom.
- Church for marginalised groups: contrary to the instincts of the Christendom era, those on the margins should receive priority attention from God's people.

- Indigenous neighbourhood churches: grass-roots strategies are consistent with the biblical story. Subversive missional approaches will be preferable in post-Christendom churches to imperialistic invitational models.
- Churches shaped by community engagement: the Christendom church was a dominant social institution, shaping culture rather than responding to cultural changes. Post-Christendom will require a more responsive approach.
- Organic church: post-Christendom churches will need simpler expressions of community, often in domestic settings, and less institutional paraphernalia.
- Alternative worship: multi-voiced participation, consensual leadership and community hermeneutics may be more helpful for post-Christendom church than more popular features of alt.worship.
- New monasticism: rules of life and rhythms of worship may be essential to sustain communities of resident aliens in post-Christendom.

Whether some emerging churches eventually develop into post-Christendom churches may depend on whether they avoid obsession with the challenge of postmodernity and grapple with the more fundamental challenge of post-Christendom.

Whatever they become, we may find emerging churches as disturbing, unsettling and threatening as Peter's visit to Cornelius was to the Jerusalem church. It is bad enough to know that initiatives are underway that threaten our convictions and seem like implicit criticisms of inherited churches. It is harder when (as in Peter's vision) the initiatives challenge our understanding of God's mission and breach our boundaries. It is harder still when our suspicion grows that they may be Spirit-inspired initiatives.

It does not help when those who report on developments blame God! 'The Spirit told me' (Acts 11:12); 'the Holy Spirit came on them' (v. 15); 'God gave them the same gift he gave us' (v. 17). This has been the lingua franca of ecclesial and missional pioneers throughout history, but it is hard to know how to respond – especially when the clinching argument is 'who was I to think that I could oppose God?' (v. 17).

Actually, this language is rarely used within emerging churches. Most are self-critical, cautious and receptive to challenge. The humble, self-deprecating attitude apparent in many (if not all) emerging churches is refreshing and bodes well for the emergence of post-Christendom ecumenism as well as post-Christendom churches.

Will church after Christendom *emerge*? Is the current wave of emerging churches the first stage? The evidence currently available is inconclusive, but emerging churches highlight missional and ecclesial issues church after Christendom must confront.

But perhaps church after Christendom will *evolve* from inherited churches that have negotiated previous paradigm shifts. The shift from Christendom to post-Christendom may be the most challenging since the fourth-century shift from pre-Christendom to Christendom, but inherited churches may have the courage, imagination and resources to negotiate it. This is the subject chapter 4 will investigate before returning again to Peter's conversation in Jerusalem.

4

Church After Christendom: Will It Evolve?

Hope for Inherited Church?

Christians in inherited churches react variously to news of emerging churches. Some are intrigued and press for further information. Some value the courageous pioneering evident in emerging churches. Some are impressed by the creative remixing of ancient and postmodern components in worship and experiment with this themselves. Others find offensive the implicit or explicit critique of inherited churches. They regard these ecclesial innovations as distractions from serious discipleship and sustained missional engagement with a challenging context. They suspect emerging churches are parasitic, recruiting only Christians who are disenchanted with inherited churches.

In particular, some question whether emerging churches can:

- Attain dynamic balance between worship, community and mission.
- Transform the ethos, not just the shape and style, of churches.
- Sustain faith and discipleship beyond one generation.
- Foster mature communities that can transcend initial homogeneity.

- Avoid drifting back into institutional mode and default ecclesial models.
- Reach the pre-churched and anti-churched as well as de-churched, semi-churched and post-churched.

Chapter 3 concluded it is too soon to judge whether this ecclesial turbulence will lead to the emergence of church after Christendom. Such a church must be able to survive the difficult years ahead, tell and live out the Jesus story faithfully, sustain the faith of exiles and embrace fresh opportunities as Christendom disintegrates. Church after Christendom may *emerge* (from this or another wave of ecclesial reconfiguration), but it might also *evolve* from inherited churches.

Can inherited churches negotiate transition into post-Christendom? Their long history, capacity to evolve to meet past challenges and cultural changes, rich traditions and resources, considerable numerical strength despite ongoing decline, deep roots in many communities and experienced leadership may appear to offer greater hope than marginal emerging churches. Some are confident they can negotiate this transition as they have negotiated others. Ann Morisy, for instance, insists: 'the Church is incredibly resilient to have weathered the storms for two millennia ... nothing the Church has to face today can match the traumas' of the past.[1]

But post-Christendom is a new and very different challenge; inherited churches may not adjust sufficiently or quickly enough. They are rooted in Christendom structures, assumptions, strategies, priorities and ways of thinking. The Christendom DNA shapes their responses. Graham Cray writes:

---

[1] Ann Morisy, *Journeying Out: A New Approach to Christian Mission* (London: Morehouse, 2004), 1.

All the major church traditions in this country have been shaped by Christendom – by an expectation that they have a special right to be heard and that people "ought" to listen to them. Whole strategies of evangelism have been based on a residual guilt about not going to church. But we are now one voice among many.[2]

And Morisy acknowledges: 'we cannot rely on previous habits and structures to help us cope, let alone flourish in such unfamiliar terrain.'[3]

This is true not only of long-established congregations and denominations but also of younger churches and networks, some of which assume with a mixture of arrogance and naïveté that they are not infected by the Christendom virus and are well-placed for the future. In fact, many new churches are more deeply and obliviously in thrall to Christendom attitudes than older churches, which at least understand the issues all churches in Western culture are facing. Superficial attempts to rebrand inherited church without making real changes are not encouraging. More than this will be needed for inherited churches to evolve into church after Christendom.

Some present evidence that inherited churches are thriving. Cathedral congregations across Britain are growing; some are even adding new congregations to cope with demand. Many interpret this as indicating a yearning for mystery and transcendence rather than informality. Traditional services in multi-congregational churches sustain existing members and attract others. Some programme- driven modernist churches, offering pre-packaged theo- logy and unremittingly joyful choruses,

[2] Graham Cray, *Youth Congregations and the Emerging Church* (Cambridge: Grove, 2002), 9.
[3] Morisy, *Journeying*, 230.

are flourishing. Charismatic fundamentalism, large-church anonymity and unchanging high-church liturgy still nourish some people in this transitional era. And encouraging signs of life and hope are evident in many ordinary churches throughout the country. Despite decline and struggle, inherited churches still make enormous contributions to many of the most deprived and divided communities. Alongside discouraging reports of many people leaving inherited churches, others are finding faith and joining them.

Maybe, however, we should not place unwarranted confidence in the persistence and apparent health of inherited churches. Burgeoning modernist churches may be refuges temporarily holding at bay contemporary cultural challenges. They may cater for the longing for certainty and fixed dogma in a time of change, but this is often backward-looking and escapist. The growth of cathedral congregations may reflect a yearning for stability in a changing society or undemanding spectatorism in a post-commitment era (a form of 'believing without belonging').[4] Traditional services may still nurture those for whom Christendom persists and even connect with the final generation of de-churched and semi-churched people whose childhood memories of church these services rekindle. But these forms of church may not thrive in post-Christendom.

Nevertheless, in some quarters, hope burns brightly that many inherited churches can evolve to meet the challenges of a changing culture. Many welcomed enthusiastically the publication in 2002 of *Hope for the Church*, in which Bob Jackson urges Anglican churches to learn from best practice

---

[4] How much does the growth of cathedral congregations owe to people leaving other churches and opting for a less demanding form of church? See further Thomas, *Counting*, 98–105.

and develop strategies for church growth.[5] This carefully researched book presents evidence of alarming decline in almost all aspects of inherited church. But Jackson identifies churches that are bucking these trends and lessons others can learn from them. Recognising the significance of contextual factors he wisely does not distil these into a single model or programme. But he advocates principles and practices that may help churches face into the future with greater confidence.

Jackson's book has a preface by Robert Warren, whose own books have helped many to face the challenge of building missionary congregations.[6] Warren acknowledges the magnitude of the shift in most inherited churches from pastoral orientation to mission orientation. He recognises this journey may take years and warns against bolting on missional activities without tackling the church's underlying ethos. But he encourages inherited churches to embark on this journey. Warren concedes that new churches may sometimes be necessary, but his writings are primarily directed towards the missional evolution of inherited churches.

Many other books and resources assume that the way forward into post-Christendom is for inherited churches to evolve, adapt, transition and reinvent themselves, as they have done in previous periods of cultural change. The great majority of Christians still belong to inherited churches, so dismissing their contribution and abandoning hope for them seems premature. There is as yet no evidence that the

---

[5] Bob Jackson, *Hope for the Church: Contemporary Strategies for Growth* (London: Church House, 2002).

[6] Robert Warren, *Being Human, Being Church: Spirituality and Mission in the Local Church* (London: Marshall Pickering, 1995) and *Building Missionary Congregations* (London: Church House, 1995).

future will belong to emerging churches (the present wave or any future wave); nor have those who have left inherited churches yet demonstrated their capacity to regroup, thrive or even survive over the long haul.

However, inherited churches face enormous challenges and many strategies proposed for their evolution seem not to appreciate the paradigm shift required for them to have a future in post-Christendom. The falling numbers and disintegrating denominational structures many churches are experiencing or will shortly encounter will require more radical action. The concept of post-Christendom (which produced blank looks in the 1990s) is becoming familiar, but it seems few yet understand the significance of the demise of Christendom.

Hope for the Church, for instance, has a chapter on 'The Church after Christendom', but this merely acknowledges the demise of Christendom and the need for different strategies. There is no engagement with the Christendom legacy and its implications for church after Christendom. Likewise, Michael Nazir-Ali, in *Shapes of the Church to Come*, recognises the church may be entering a period of exile and must prepare for this but urges the inherited church to 'value its established role for as long as it lasts'.[7] These authors accept the end of Christendom, often with regret, but seem to believe post-Christendom will be an attenuated version of the past rather than a different era.[8]

If church after Christendom is to evolve, a trenchant critique of the ethos, mindset and legacy of Christendom is vital. Inherited churches may find resources in the dissident tradition that over the centuries developed such a critique. This tradition is sometimes unappreciative of the

---

[7] Michael Nazir-Ali, *Shapes of the Church to Come* (Eastbourne: Kingsway, 2001), 200.

[8] See further, Murray, *Post-Christendom*, 206–16.

positive dimensions of the Christendom era, but it is a helpful counterbalance to unexamined inherited church assumptions. There are signs that this critique is beginning to be heeded.[9] Disavowal of Christendom is a vital precondition for the evolution of post-Christendom churches.

Evolving or Emerging?

So, will church after Christendom evolve or emerge? And if the latter, are churches presently emerging around the edges of inherited church the first fruits of church after Christendom?

Practitioners and observers respond variously to these questions. Some, as we have seen, believe inherited churches can embrace the paradigm shift and evolve into post-Christendom churches. Others are less sanguine. Michael Moynagh, for instance, affirms the continuing role of inherited churches and endorses Jackson's plea that we should learn from best practice. He points to specific factors in the 1990s that exacerbated decline, so we should not assume the rate of decline will necessarily continue in the present decade. But he endorses emerging churches as the primary source of hope and urges denominational leaders to invest heavily in resourcing them.[10]

This is also the position of Michael Frost and Alan Hirsch, who write:

---

[9] There are hints of this in *Mission-shaped Church* (London: Church House, 2004) and a commentary on this report: George Lings and Bob Hopkins, *Mission-shaped Church: The Inside and Outside View* (Encounters on the Edge No.22; Sheffield: The Sheffield Centre, 2004).

[10] In a session for Churches Together in England (17 September 2003). See further Michael Moynagh, *emergingchurch.intro* (Oxford: Monarch, 2004).

the planting of new, culturally diverse, missional communities is the best way forward for the church ... While some established churches can be revitalized, success seems to be rare from our experience and perspective ... the real hope lies with those courageous leaders who will foster the development of alternative, experimental, new communities of faith.[11]

Even the ecumenical *Building Bridges of Hope* process, which accompanies emerging and evolving churches, notes with concern: 'the best efforts of those using traditional patterns of engaging, nurture and enablement seem to be doing little more than slow down the decline.'[12]

Whether the current wave of emerging churches – or at least some expressions of this diverse phenomenon – can justify the hopes some are investing in them will not be known for some time. Most emerging church practitioners do not make exaggerated claims about what is happening. They are rightly wary of placing an unhelpful weight of expectation on young initiatives. This typically postmodern reticence is a welcome change from 'this-is-the-answer' advocacy of models and strategies that has plagued churches in recent years. But we should not underestimate the seriousness, even desperation, of many Christians in emerging churches, praying and working for ecclesial and missional transformation.

Nor, though, should we underestimate the influence of reactivity in some emerging churches and the struggle to move from this into proactive and creative missiology and ecclesiology. This is a particular problem in emerging churches shaped by the concerns of post-evangelical, post-charismatic and post-churched people. Whether

---

[11] Frost and Hirsch, *Shaping*, x.
[12] *Building Bridges of Hope* (Stage B) findings. See further www.ctbi.org.uk/bbh.

'recovery churches' can become vibrant missional communities is uncertain: this may be a paradigm shift as great as
inherited churches face at the end of Christendom. Graham
Cray doubts, for example, that 'post-evangelicals hold the
key to the future shape of the church. It is much more likely
that it will be the following generation, that live beyond the
"hinge" between cultural eras ... who will discover the way
forward.'[13]

We might also ask if emerging churches have addressed
any more effectively than inherited churches the necessary
disavowal of Christendom. *The Shaping of Things to Come*
by Michael Frost and Alan Hirsch, which will inspire and
resource emerging churches, addresses this issue and hopefully will put it on the agenda for many. But the
overwhelming concern within emerging churches thus far
has been to reconfigure church in light of the shift from
modernity to postmodernity. Postmodernity, though, is
only one (albeit important) dimension of the paradigm shift
from Christendom to post-Christendom. Postmodern
churches, whatever shape these take, may not be adequately
equipped for post-Christendom.

The survey of emerging churches in chapter 3 concluded
that the jury remains out on their significance and
sustainability, but emerging churches highlight missional
and ecclesial issues that churches after Christendom will
need to confront.

Evolving and Emerging

Perhaps the way forward lies neither with inherited
nor with emerging church, but in a partnership between

---

[13] Graham Cray et al., *The Post-evangelical Debate* (London:
Triangle, 1997), 7.

different expressions of church. The authors of *Mission-shaped Church* welcome Archbishop Rowan Williams' encouragement of 'mixed-economy' approaches and his support for those exploring fresh 'ways of being church alongside the inherited parochial pattern'.[14] This dual endorsement can be dismissed as a political manoeuvre to keep everyone happy, but it may signify much more than this.

Negotiating the transition from Christendom to post-Christendom will involve both evolution and emergence. A mutually respectful relationship between emerging and inherited churches, involving open and patient dialogue, could produce a symbiotic partnership that offers greater hope for the future than isolation or competition.

Inherited churches need the stimulus of emerging churches. Dissident movements and alternative churches have always been irritating and threatening to inherited churches, which during the Christendom era marginalised and persecuted most of them. But the core values and distinctive practices of many groups gradually permeated inherited churches and brought renewal. Inherited churches have benefited from the experience of church planters and other pioneering initiatives during the late twentieth century. Emerging churches offer further resources – not for uncritical adoption or superficial imitation, but for reflection and growth.

Emerging churches need the wisdom, historical perspective and resources of inherited churches. The present paradigm shift may pose new challenges, but there are parallels with previous generations in which churches faced significant cultural changes. From the failures and successes of such encounters they can learn valuable lessons. And the

---

[14] *Mission-Shaped Church*, 26 (quoting from the foreword to a report to the Church in Wales).

tried and trusted liturgical patterns and theological resources of inherited churches can save emerging churches from unnecessary and exhausting innovation, unbalanced and unhealthy emphases and self-imposed ecclesial poverty. Uncritical adoption is no more helpful in this direction than the other, but emerging churches will surely benefit from discerning appropriation of inherited church resources.

Learning from inherited churches

There are already encouraging signs that emerging churches are valuing inherited church traditions. New monastic movements are reappropriating and reconfiguring ancient forms of mission, community and spirituality. Alt.worship often involves creative blending of ancient and contemporary elements, as post-charismatics and post-evangelicals rediscover liturgical treasures ignored or denigrated by churches from which they have decamped. The danger, typical of postmodern culture, is irresponsible eclecticism, unwittingly importing Christendom assumptions that may hinder the emergence of post-Christendom churches.

Some emerging churches are particularly inspired by Celtic Christianity, embracing its creation-oriented spirituality, refreshing liturgies, flexible ecclesial structures and indigenising approach to mission within culture.[15] Celtic Christianity has renewed and nurtured many people, in and beyond emerging churches, but some aspects of it may be problematic in post-Christendom – in particular, its top-down missiology and very limited engagement with the life and teaching of Jesus.

---

[15] See Gerard Kelly, *Retrofuture: Rediscovering Our Roots, Recharting Our Routes* (Downers Grove: InterVarsity Press, 1999), 185–6 for a helpful summary of the appeal of Celtic Christianity in emerging churches.

Other emerging churches look further back to the early churches, encouraged by the writings of Robert Webber, whose concept of *ancient-future faith* undergirds their liturgical experimentation. Webber argues:

> it may be broadly said that the story of Christianity moves from a focus on mystery in the classical period, to institution in the medieval era, to individualism in the Reformation era, to reason in the modern era, and now, in the postmodern era, back to mystery.[16]

Pre-Christendom liturgical, ethical and missional resources (appropriately contextualised) may be very helpful for emerging post-Christendom churches, since they do not carry the Christendom virus that traditions from later centuries do.

Perhaps this is why some emerging churches find the Anabaptist tradition inspiring. As a story-rich tradition, deeply committed to mission and community, located on the margins and critical of the Christendom system, Anabaptism offers ways of thinking and core values many have embraced. However, Anabaptism is stronger on being counter-cultural than being culturally attuned: this may be a corrective to the opposite tendency in some emerging churches, but this feature may make Anabaptism less immediately attractive.[17]

But there are also within mainstream Christendom traditions resources that will enrich emerging churches.

---

[16] Robert E. Webber, *Ancient-Future Faith: Rethinking Evangelicalism for a Postmodern World* (Grand Rapids: Baker, 1999), 16.

[17] Those who draw on any of these movements, however, must beware the temptations of projection, romanticism and wish-fulfilment.

Post-Christendom churches will emerge on stronger foundations if they understand the Christendom legacy and make conscious and principled choices about what to adopt from the past and what to dispense with. Furthermore, interaction between emerging and inherited churches need not be limited to appropriation of past practices and liturgical material. Conversations, friendships, joint activities, spiritual direction and mentoring can all enable emerging churches to draw on the wisdom and experience of inherited churches.

Learning from emerging churches

There are also signs of pioneering initiatives in emerging churches stimulating inherited churches. The positive reception accorded to the *Mission-shaped Church* report within and beyond Anglican circles and the interest of many denominations in emerging church indicates that listening has begun and that prospects are good for learning from what is developing.

But there are dangers. Subjecting young emerging churches to excessive scrutiny, introducing new components into inherited churches without considering contextual factors, cherry-picking interesting practices without understanding their significance, searching for 'answers' but not wrestling with missiological questions – insensitive and superficial responses will damage emerging and inherited churches and jeopardise the listening and learning that will benefit inherited churches.

This should not stop inherited churches from experimenting. Introducing café-style events or incorporating elements of alt.worship, for instance, will not produce post-Christendom churches. But this may stimulate journeys of discovery that will enable inherited churches to reflect more deeply on issues of culture and identify areas for further ecclesial and missional development. Experimentation, however, is not the only response. The critique of inherited church in some emerging churches is sharp and inherited churches may find this hard to receive; but it may help them understand why people are leaving their churches.

The symbiotic relationship envisaged here will require patient two-way listening. There are dangers with listening processes – endless analysis, domestication and dilution of radical ideas, distraction from action, critical and judgemental attitudes, and entrenched reactions. But far greater are the dangers of not listening in a plural culture where no one expression of church can incarnate the gospel effectively. Listening may enable post-Christendom churches to both evolve and emerge in ways that would not be possible without this interaction.

Inherited and Emerging

Contrasting 'emerging' and 'inherited' church is useful for the purpose of analysis but misleading. All churches are both inherited and emerging. Leith Anderson comments wryly:

> A conservative guess is that 98% of our behaviour is rooted in one tradition or another. Those who operate at the 99% level are considered to be the old-fashioned traditionalists, and those who operate at the 97% level are called avant-garde nontraditionalists. It is mostly a matter of degree.[18]

Nobody starts with a totally blank canvas. Everyone operates from within an inherited tradition, however we critique

---

[18] Leith Anderson, *Church for the 21st Century* (Grand Rapids: Bethany House, 1992), 146.

and reshape what we have received. The most radical church planting or emerging church initiatives reconfigure inherited ways of thinking about mission, worship and community. Michael Nazir-Ali comments:

> Something essential in the nature of the church influences, indeed determines, its shape in every age and every culture. However responsive the church may be to outside pressures, there is an internal dynamic that must be taken into account.[19]

One way of classifying emerging churches distinguishes three kinds of emergence, some of which are closer than others to inherited churches:

- Churches emerging *from* inherited church through processes of renewal and transformation. The outcome is not another church but a church more or less radically different from the past in structure, ethos, style, focus or activities.
- Churches emerging *out of* inherited church through processes of community engagement, liturgical exploration, church planting or missional reflection. The outcome is a new (or embryonic) church that becomes more or less autonomous.
- Churches emerging *within* a particular context without the shaping influence of or significant connection to inherited church. The outcome is a new church, which may be more or less radical, that will need to build links with other churches.

Furthermore, even the most traditional inherited churches are emerging, for different people are involved in succeeding generations who shape the traditions in new ways, and

---

[19] Nazir-Ali, *Shapes*, 41.

no church is entirely unaffected by cultural changes happening around it. Indeed, unless we arrogantly claim our understanding and practice is perfect, we will always strive to continue emerging into churches that more adequately reflect the glory of Christ and embody the values and priorities of his kingdom.

What we need, then, are not formal consultations between official representatives of inherited and emerging churches, as if either were distinct or homogeneous groupings. Mutual defensiveness, incomprehension and limited benefits will accrue from such processes (as was the case with meetings in the 1980s between official representatives of the 'mainline' denominations and the New Churches). We need multidirectional conversations, based on mutual respect, aware that all churches face the challenge of rediscovering how to be church on the margins in post-Christendom. We need each other!

Stories are being shared. Consultations, reports and books are introducing emerging churches to inherited churches.[20] Websites offer opportunities for story-sharing and debate.[21] Cliff College organised a 'Shape of Future Church' conference in January 2004 and has another planned for 2005. Denominational and ecumenical bodies are sponsoring and accompanying emerging churches. *Building Bridges of Hope* involves both evolving and emerging churches, drawing representatives together for annual conferences. An interesting cross-section of people from inherited and emerging churches participated in 'The Future of the People of God' conference in July 2004.

---

[20] The bibliography lists books on the emerging church. See further many footnotes in chapter 3 and a more extensive bibliography in Murray, *Changing Mission*.

[21] See, especially www.emergingchurch.info and www.opensourcetheology.net.

But there is room for more:

- Conversations between groups exploring *similar* models of emerging church can enable them to learn from each other's experiences. Emerging churches committed to small-scale church, for instance, can explore the strengths and weaknesses of cell church, household church, table church and small Christian communities.
- Conversations between groups exploring *different* models of emerging church can help each value what others bring. Emerging churches oriented towards worship, for example, can engage with those oriented towards community or mission.
- Conversations between groups reconfiguring inherited models of church, such as purpose-driven or seeker-oriented churches, and churches emerging in other contexts can help each appreciate advantages and drawbacks.
- Conversations between inherited churches and various emerging churches can offer fresh insights that spark the imagination of inherited churches, helping them re-examine what they are doing and why.
- Conversations between emerging churches and various inherited churches can expose emerging churches to the concerns and questions of inherited churches and encourage them to consider these issues.

Peter's conversation with the Jerusalem church in Acts 11 is an encouraging example of the kind of open and discerning conversations we need today. The key elements are story-telling, theological reflection, critical questioning, careful listening, passionate advocacy and thoughtful conclusion.

Peter represented the very early stages of an emerging church among Gentiles, a development that stretched his own understanding of God, church and mission. The Jerusalem church, though still young, was the guardian of the tradition, responsible for scrutinising Peter's possibly irresponsible pioneering activities.

Peter's disturbing story provoked questions and sharp criticisms, but the conclusion of the passage indicates these were open-ended; the Jerusalem church did not prejudge the issues. As indicated previously, in many ways the challenge was harder for the church than for Peter. He had been there and was convinced that God was at work; they had only Peter's report. And there were massive cultural, strategic and theological issues at stake. But they listened well, weighed up what they heard and discerned signs of the Spirit in Peter's story.

Peter gladly made himself accountable to the Jerusalem church, not apologetically or anticipating rejection, but telling his story with conviction and trusting his friends and colleagues to assess it wisely and fairly. They were not afraid to express concerns and question him vigorously, but they endorsed his actions, even eating with Gentiles, and despite their discomfort they thanked God. Subsequently, Paul would admonish Peter for his reluctance to eat with Gentile believers.[22] Even after his experience in Cornelius' home, Peter still struggled with this paradigm shift – the Jerusalem church in Acts 11 did remarkably well!

We should not read this incident as suggesting that conversations between emerging and inherited churches always involve pioneers justifying initiatives before representatives of inherited churches. *Mutual* accountability, rooted in friendship and trust, is vital for multidirectional listening on the cusp of post-Christendom. But often the experiences of

---

[22] Galatians 2:11–12.

emerging church pioneers will prompt the most animated discussion; this biblical encounter indicates the spirit in which such conversations can take place and holds out the prospect of encouraging outcomes.

What might such conversations achieve?

- Inherited churches might adopt or adapt helpful perspectives and practices from emerging churches.
- Emerging churches might learn from history and avoiding repeating mistakes.
- Inherited churches might recognise and renounce attitudes and practices that damage their witness and disable their own members.
- Emerging churches might rediscover and release the radical potential of familiar church practices.
- Emerging and inherited churches might think more deeply about themselves and their local context.
- Cross-fertilising between different emerging churches might benefit each or even produce healthy hybrids.
- Inherited and emerging churches might forge mutually enriching partnerships.
- New churches might emerge from, or out of, inherited churches.
- Inherited and emerging churches might be better equipped for the challenges and opportunities of post-Christendom.

Evolving, Emerging and Global

The conversation between Peter and the Jerusalem church resulted from his visit to the home of someone from another culture. The Jerusalem church discovered that it now belonged within an ethnically more diverse church than it had previously imagined. Initially threatening, this unexpected development breathed new life into the Jewish churches. Despite theological and cultural misgivings, they authorised mission to the Gentiles, refused to impose burdensome customs on Gentile believers and embraced a paradigm shift that would lead to Gentile churches far outnumbering Jewish churches. Already within the New Testament, Gentile churches were sending financial aid to the hard-pressed Jerusalem church, repaying their debt for the gift of the gospel.[23]

During the past forty years the church in Britain has become ethnically more diverse than previous generations could have imagined, expressed through ethnically mixed congregations and mono-ethnic churches. Some celebrate this diversity, the new life that has infused inherited churches and the planting of new churches in inner-city areas from which most inherited churches had withdrawn. Others find this diversity threatening, especially when the influx of Christians from other cultures changes the culture of 'their' church. Some query the legitimacy of mono-ethnic churches, especially in local communities fractured along ethnic lines. Others admit that many inherited churches are ethnically homogeneous and that some supposedly mono-ethnic churches are culturally diverse. Some struggle to build multicultural rather than merely multi-ethnic churches. Others concentrate on building friendship and partnership between different churches.

The size and proliferation of mono-ethnic churches, together with the influx into inherited churches of Christians from many cultures, has transformed ecclesial demographics, especially in the cities. In London today fewer than half of those who attend church regularly are white.[24] Some mono-ethnic churches are by far the largest

---

[23] 2 Corinthians 8–10.
[24] Brierley, *Tide*, 139.

churches in their area. Many others are the only expression of church on a housing estate. Some concentrate on people from one ethnic or linguistic group. Others want to develop multicultural churches from a non-white base. Several networks and denominations link together some mono-ethnic churches, although many are independent and new churches are constantly emerging.

These developments are encouraging. They intercept the disillusionment and weariness of many declining Western churches. For many they are hopeful signs. The incorporation of mono-ethnic churches into mainstream denominations has boosted numbers and invigorated denominational gatherings (although disguising the rate of decline otherwise underway). The anticipated growth and further proliferation of mono-ethnic churches, possibly enhanced by the immigration into Western nations of more Christians from the global South, might partially offset the shrinkage of inherited churches. But mono-ethnic churches will face struggles in the years ahead as their next generation rejects mono-ethnic culture, as the influence of secularisation bites, and as they attempt to develop more holistic and incarnational models of mission.

Another development has been the arrival of missionaries from former 'receiving nations' to evangelise the 'sending nations' from whom they received the gospel in previous generations. The globalisation of mission has made such terminology anachronistic as missionaries from Africa, Latin America and Asia come to Europe. Some work in mono-ethnic contexts, others in or alongside inherited churches.

These developments are further nails in the coffin of Western Christendom, although they do not preclude the emergence of new Christendoms elsewhere.[25] They may be

---

[25] See Murray, *Post-Christendom*, 14–17, 187, and Philip Jenkins, *The Next Christendom: The Coming of Global Christianity* (New York: Oxford University Press, 2002).

deeply significant for the emergence or evolution of post-Christendom churches. Conversations between inherited and emerging churches, therefore, should embrace mono-ethnic churches and missionaries from other nations.

Several factors may hinder such conversations. Inherited churches are strongest in suburban and provincial communities, geographically and culturally distant from areas where mono-ethnic churches flourish. Emerging churches are overwhelmingly white and more concerned about postmodernity than multicultural issues. Although inherited and emerging churches today dissociate themselves from the overt and institutional racism that partly precipitated the emergence of mono-ethnic churches, Eurocentric assumptions about theology, church, mission, culture and ethics are painfully evident to non-white Christians.

Another issue is the influence of Christendom perspectives and practices. Western missionaries exported the ideology and accoutrements of Christendom, assuming that these were Christian. Some mono-ethnic churches and missionaries from these nations are importing these perspectives and practices back into Western societies: hierarchical and authoritarian leadership, charismatic fundamentalism, tithing and prosperity teaching, approaches to biblical interpretation and evangelism, and much else. Inherited and emerging churches, now more sensitive to such issues and looking to develop post-Christendom alternatives, may struggle to engage with mono-ethnic churches imbued with Christendom presuppositions.

But such conversations are essential to enhance missiological understanding, build strategic alliances and catalyse imaginative and courageous expressions of church after Christendom.

- Conversations between inherited, emerging and mono-ethnic churches might remind us that the centre of gravity of the world church is not in the West but the South. Neither evolution nor emergence of church after Christendom in Western culture is guaranteed. But the continuing decline of Western churches – even their virtual eradication – will not jeopardise global mission. This sense of perspective is important.
- Such conversations might prompt discussion about the continued hegemony of inherited Western churches, which assume that their expressions of spirituality, theological views and ethical stances are normative. The continued dominance of Western churches (despite 'partnership' language) in global denominations, mission agencies and Christian organisations is becoming obnoxious.
- Conversations between emerging and mono-ethnic churches (and missionaries from other nations) might challenge emerging churches to transcend their designation as 'the emerging church in the white, Anglo, postmodern, post-Christian subculture'.[26] Emerging churches are a Western phenomenon; they are responses to post-Christendom and postmodernity. But their development will be stunted and their impact limited without greater ethnic diversity. White Christians alone cannot incarnate the gospel in multi-ethnic post-Christendom.
- Conversations between missionaries from other nations, Western missiologists and inherited

---

[26] Matthew Glock's phrase. See www.emergingchurch.info/reflection/matthewglock/index.htm.

churches might identify barriers preventing inherited churches from engaging effectively with multi-ethnic communities. They might also help the missionaries understand more deeply the culture in which they now live and why evangelism is harder than in their own nation.

- Such conversations might also help inherited churches decide which models and strategies might be useful in a Western context. Appreciating contextual factors might dissuade them from adopting unsuitable programmes and raising unrealistic expectations. They might also become more aware of the resources of the world church.

- Conversations between mono-ethnic, inherited and emerging churches might foster creative strategies for incarnating the gospel in particular communities in ways that embody both cultural diversity and ecclesial unity.

Symbiosis

The brightest hope for church after Christendom is a symbiotic relationship between inherited and emerging (including mono-ethnic) churches.[27] We need each other. We need creative partnerships and new forms of ecumenism. We need to listen to those walking through the front and back doors of various churches. We need to grapple with multiple configurations of believing and belonging (and behaving) in post-Christendom. Church after Christendom will both evolve and emerge. Emerging, mono-ethnic and inherited churches face common challenges:

---

[27] A symbiotic relationship involves two organisms interacting together for the benefit of both.

- How do churches in a diverse and changing culture maintain creative tension between being 'culturally attuned' and 'counter-cultural'?
- In a post-commitment culture, are high-commitment models needed, or low-commitment models?
- How homogeneous are most inherited and emerging churches, and how can we pursue the eschatological vision of a multicultural church?
- Within which networks and subcultures are neither inherited nor emerging churches represented?
- Are churches developing inter-generational strategies to pass on the faith in a culture where the Christian story and its values are becoming alien?
- Will distaste for inherited models of evangelism discourage all evangelism, or will new – and effective – expressions emerge?
- How can evangelical and charismatic churches nurture divergent as well as convergent thinkers towards mature discipleship, and how can other churches attract converts?
- How can churches balance deeply held core convictions and space for open-ended questions, diversity and mystery?
- What can inherited and emerging churches learn from the worldwide recovery of small-scale church?
- How can accountable risk-taking (Acts 11) transcend both safety-first church culture and maverick irresponsibility?

We can also listen across the centuries. Both inherited and emerging churches need historical perspectives as well as global perspectives. Whatever emerges or evolves will have features of both continuity and discontinuity with the past.

Inherited churches *seem* historically aware and connected to the past, but many are ignorant of their own history and stuck in recent traditions that hinder the recovery of life-giving resources. Some are located so squarely within evangelical, charismatic, liberal, contemplative, Anglo-catholic or other traditions that they struggle to access resources from other traditions. But church after Christendom requires reconfiguration that crosses boundaries and draws on the richest resources from many traditions.

Emerging churches also need historical perspectives lest they become disoriented, exhausted by innovating or over-burdened by their own significance. They need the resources of the past, but must resist the temptation to indulge in shallow and eclectic historical pillaging. They need to take time to understand the significance and inter-connectedness of traditions handed down over generations before attempting to contextualise these into contemporary culture.

Robert Webber advocates such interaction with history. Although his main concern is with the shift from modernity to postmodernity, his comments are equally applicable to the shift from Christendom to post-Christendom.

> We now live in a transitional time ... Some leaders will insist on preserving the Christian faith in its modern form; others will run headlong into the sweeping changes that accommodate Christianity to postmodern forms; and a third group will carefully and cautiously seek to interface historic Christian truths into the dawning of a new era.[28]

Church history is a wonderful treasury, but its scope is daunting. On what basis can we search for the most useful resources? Four possible criteria are:

- Antiquity – digging down to the deepest roots of the church, hoping that the oldest sources are purest.

---

[28] Webber, *Ancient-Future*, 14.

Post-Christendom is not pre-Christendom, but churches in the first three centuries were marginal communities in a plural society, from which we can learn much.

- Marginality – emerging from Christendom, we can learn from marginal groups, once dismissed and persecuted, whose perspectives now seem more pertinent than those of their mainstream opponents.
- Similarity – negotiating the shift into post-Christendom, we can learn from previous generations of Christians who negotiated other culture shifts, taking encouragement and heeding warnings.
- Continuity – investigating the roots of our own denomination or church is inspiring and transformational. It is also an effective response in inherited churches to the reaction: 'we've never done it this way before'.

Ethos

The second part of this book will investigate the ethos of church after Christendom. The emergence/evolution of post-Christendom churches involves not only reshaping churches for a changed and changing context but also recovering authentic ways of being church that were damaged, distorted or compromised during the Christendom era. As Brian Castle warns: 'The Church is considering "new ways of being church" … the emphasis needs to be on new ways of *being* church and not simply on new ways of *doing* church.'[29]

---

[29] Brian Castle, *Unofficial God?: Voices from Beyond the Walls* (London: SPCK, 2004), 130.

There is no hard-and-fast distinction between 'shape' and 'ethos' (any more than between 'inherited' and 'emerging'). A church's ethos affects its shape and a church's shape expresses and reinforces its ethos. But in the context of multiple expressions of church, each with passionate advocates, the temptation is strong to focus on models and styles rather than core values.[30]

Perhaps various inherited and emerging expressions of church are equally capable of embodying the core values of church after Christendom. A church's shape may deter or attract some potential joiners; but its ethos is more significant. It is certainly more significant for retaining the allegiance of potential leavers, as is clear from the issues raised by leavers.[31] Its ethos is also critical for nurturing counter-cultural discipleship and creating missional communities to incarnate the gospel creatively and winsomely in the strange new world of post-Christendom.

---

[30] Several recent books on emerging churches have this term in their title. See, for example, *Mission-Shaped Church*, Nazir-Ali, *Shapes* and Frost and Hirsch, *Shaping*.
[31] See chapter 2.

Part Two

Ethos

Prologue

The question under discussion in Part One was *how* church after Christendom might emerge or evolve; the question in Part Two is *what kind* of church can survive and flourish in post-Christendom. These questions are inter-related, of course, so we will dig deeper into issues investigated in Part One. In particular, we will probe further the link between belonging, believing and behaving, continue listening to the joiners and leavers, sift through inherited church resources and learn from the experience of emerging churches in the areas of mission, community and worship.

An immediate disclaimer is needed. The following chapters do not pretend to offer a comprehensive twenty-first century ecclesiology! They offer contributions from a particular angle to the quest for expressions of church that may be sustainable and effective after Christendom. The post-Christendom lens helps us focus on aspects of church the Christendom shift distorted or marginalised. Perpetuating distortions may import damaging practices into post-Christendom churches; ignoring marginalised elements may deprive them of vital processes and resources.[1]

---

[1] Later books in the *After Christendom* series will address other ecclesial issues than those explored here.

Our biblical reference point in Part Two is a remarkable description of the processes by which churches grow to maturity.

> As a prisoner for the Lord, then, I urge you to live a life worthy of the calling you have received. Be completely humble and gentle; be patient, bearing with one another in love. Make every effort to keep the unity of the Spirit through the bond of peace. There is one body and one Spirit – just as you were called to one hope when you were called – one Lord, one faith, one baptism; one God and Father of all, who is over all and through all and in all.
>
> But to each one of us grace has been given as Christ apportioned it. This is why it says: "When he ascended on high, he led captives in his train and gave gifts to people." (What does 'he ascended' mean except that he also descended to the lower, earthly regions? He who descended is the very one who ascended higher than all the heavens, in order to fill the whole universe.)
>
> It was he who gave some to be apostles, some to be prophets, some to be evangelists, and some to be pastors and teachers, to prepare God's people for works of service, so that the body of Christ may be built up until we all reach unity in the faith and in the knowledge of the Son of God and become mature, attaining to the whole measure of the fulness of Christ.
>
> Then we will no longer be infants, tossed back and forth by the waves, and blown here and there by every wind of teaching and by the cunning and craftiness of people in their deceitful scheming. Instead, speaking the truth in love, we will in all things grow up into him who is the Head, that is, Christ. From him the whole body, joined and held together by every supporting ligament, grows and builds itself up in love, as each part does its work.
>
> (Ephesians 4:1-16)[2]

---

[2] Most scholars reject the insertion of a comma after 'God's people' (restricting 'works of service' to those who do the preparing).

The demise of Christendom has been accompanied by uncertainty about the state of the church and its prospects in Western societies. Will it survive? Can it reinvent itself for a changing context? Is the current decline in numbers and influence terminal?

Some doubt there will be a church after Christendom. Others anticipate an attenuated, ghostly existence for the church as a relic of a fading culture. Respected sociologists predict the continuing secularisation of our culture or proclaim 'the death of Christian Britain'.[3] Popular contemporary novelists, in powerful and beautifully crafted stories, envision a post-Christian future that has reverted to paganism or embraced mysticism or materialism.[4] Some church leavers are equally pessimistic.

The *After Christendom* series assumes the church *can* outlive Christendom but does not take this for granted. It offers no simplistic strategy for church after Christendom. It shares much of the critique of church leavers and popular novelists, but argues that we can differentiate the Christendom system from dynamic Christianity. It celebrates the end of the former and possible re-emergence of the latter. Church after Christendom, if we negotiate this transition, will be marginal, in exilic mode, journeying towards a different way of being God's people in a strange new world. Discovering a new way of being church – not a revival of an old way – is the hoped-for future towards which the series points.

---

[3] For example, Bruce, *God is Dead* and Brown, *Death of Christian Britain*.

[4] For example, Philip Pullman's *His Dark Materials* trilogy and William Horwood's *The Wolves of Time* and *The Duncton Chronicles*. Both writers brilliantly portray the corruption and inherent violence of fundamentalism and Christendom-style religion.

How, then, do we work with this visionary text from Ephesians? It is a wonderful and inspiring picture of a fully functioning and loving community, where the gifts of each member are valued and contribute towards the development of a mature, healthy and Christlike church. Unity is expressed through glorious diversity. This community is neither static and moribund nor unbalanced and lurching from one idea to another, but growing spiritually and relationally. Truth is spoken in love and peace binds people together. It is Christ-centred, Spirit-energised and shares in the work and mission of God. Could this describe church after Christendom?

This text influenced the emergence of the New Churches in the 1970s and 1980s. It inspired a recovery of apostles and prophets (neglected during the Christendom era by all but dissident groups) and undergirded the development of charismatic churches in which spiritual gifts could operate. It was crucial for the movement's interpretation of New Testament ecclesiology and its hope of restoring such a church as a step towards ushering in God's kingdom and welcoming back the head of the church.

The New Churches used this passage in ways that pose problems for us. The heady expectation that the church would be restored, revival would follow and the kingdom would arrive stirred many to levels of commitment – to church and to Christ – that many beyond the movement applauded or envied. But disappointed expectations have provoked an exodus: post-charismatics from restorationist churches are strongly represented among church leavers, in post-church groups and emerging churches. The recovery of apostles and prophets, which promised to revolutionise church life, often produced structures and processes as hierarchical and disempowering as any inherited model and gradually reverted to conventional Christendom patterns (albeit with new labels). The interpretation of this passage anticipated that a restored church would exercise an influential, if not dominant, role in society and attract multitudes to its gatherings and activities.

Using this passage as our biblical reference point, therefore, is risky.[5] But there are so many resonances with the themes explored in the following chapters that (prefaced by the warnings here) the risk is worth taking. Furthermore, people in exile need a vision. Not an alluring but escapist vision of revived fortunes or return to familiar landmarks, of Christendom restored or exile quickly transcended. But a vision of what is possible in exile – and perhaps only in exile.

This was Jeremiah's contribution to the exiles in Babylon as they grieved the loss of their homeland and wondered how they could sing the Lord's song in a strange land.[6] Warning against false prophecies of imminent deliverance and restoration, he urged them to settle down and explore God's purposes for them in exile.[7] The years spent in exile transformed the people of Israel, finally ridding them of tendencies and practices that had marred their community life and witness over many centuries.

Part Two, then, will consider what aspects of church life, distorted or marginalised in the Christendom era, we might rediscover in exile. The Ephesians text will function neither as a blueprint for church after Christendom nor as the basis for painless and speedy transition to post-Christendom. But it will undergird many issues we explore and keep us rooted in the story of a church that, through the ebbs and flows of history, will finally 'in all things grow up into him who is the Head, that is, Christ'.

---

[5] Though common in books on contemporary ecclesiology, many of which are more measured in their proposals and expectations.

[6] Psalm 137.

[7] Jeremiah 29:1–9.

Church After Christendom:
Mission

Marginal Mission Movements

The church began as a marginal mission movement. Rapid growth meant that in some places, by the mid-third century, it was a socially significant community. Still committed to mission, there were nevertheless signs the movement was becoming an institution. The Christendom shift exacerbated this trend. The church moved from the margins to the centre; mission was through imposition not invitation; and church-as-movement became church-as-institution.

These developments can be interpreted as marks of success, necessary organisational maturity or sociological patterns typical of all ageing movements. But they altered the church's self-image, priorities and understanding of its societal role. An institutional church:

- Regards mission as one of many functions rather than its defining centre.
- Prioritises maintenance and designates mission to specialised agencies rather than equipping all members as missionaries.
- Interprets its mission as preservative not provocative, confirming rather than challenging the status quo.

- Expects everyone to know its language and accept without demur its cultural norms.
- Speaks and acts authoritatively and is discomforted when people choose not to belong, believe or behave in approved ways.

Such attitudes and practices will disable post-Christendom churches, hindering their essential re-formation as a marginal mission movement. Three paradigm shifts are necessary.

From Maintenance to Mission

In a context of persistent decline, renewed emphasis on mission is unsurprising. But what does this mean? How can it be accomplished? What motivates it?

This may, despite disclaimers, reflect desperation to preserve threatened institutions and reaffirm the church's social influence. We can promote evangelism and social action under the rubric of 'missional church' without disavowing the Christendom legacy. The disdain for 'mission' within some emerging churches does not enhance their prospects, but represents greater sensitivity (often without historical analysis) to the imperialistic Christendom heritage than in many inherited churches.

Mission activities have proliferated recently. High-profile initiatives include renewed emphasis on church planting, the Decade of Evangelism, *Alpha*, the *Jubilee 2000* campaign and *Faithworks*. But 'missional church' is not about bolting mission onto institutional church: a fundamental re-orientation is needed. Some of these initiatives recognised that mission originates in the character and creation-wide purposes of God, not in the church; that 'missional church' does not mean churches embracing mission more enthusiastically but encountering afresh the missionary God. Missiology in post-Christendom precedes ecclesiology, but missional theology precedes both.[1]

But these perspectives are neither widespread nor deep-rooted. The comparative ease with which mission activities can be bolted onto existing structures tempts churches to superficial responses. Predictably discouraging outcomes hinder deeper reflection and more radical action. Churches introducing cell-church or seeker-oriented strategies are discovering that restructuring does not ensure changes of mindset. A paradigm shift is required. Mission is not an agenda item – it *is* the agenda. It is not something churches do, but a divine initiative in which churches participate. Mission, not church, is the starting point.

Missional language has become familiar. But using this liberally does not guarantee missional identity and, by itself, will not ensure the development of truly missional churches.[2] Nor will desperately adopting off-the-peg 'missional church' programmes. Post-Christendom churches need a missional *ethos*, expressed in their core values and nurtured in their corporate life.

This begins with inducting newcomers into a missional mindset by, for example:

- Introducing them to the missionary God and the scope of *missio Dei*.
- Teaching them to interpret Scripture with a consistent missional hermeneutic.
- Equipping them to participate, first, in God's mission and, secondly, in church activities.

---

[1] See, above all, Bosch, *Transforming Mission*.

[2] 'In the past, churches have played with "go" language but, because they have left themselves in the centre of the frame, all such talk has been subverted once more into "come" practice': Hopkins and Lings, *Mission-shaped Church*, 19.

- Developing a process whereby they engage in missional activities and reflect on these with mentors.

But, without processes to sustain their missional ethos, newcomers and churches will revert to the default Christendom maintenance-orientation. These processes might include:

- A pattern of corporate prayer, supported by resources for private prayer, that constantly confronts the church with the broad agenda of God's mission, the needs of its local community, the systemic violence and injustice that causes global suffering, the groaning of creation and the commission to make disciples of all nations.
- Regular opportunities to reflect theologically about vocational, cultural and ethical issues, to learn to think Christianly about work-related matters and to 'prepare God's people for works of service' throughout the week. One church displays photographs of members dressed for work as reminders of their daily mission contexts; another lays hands on any starting new jobs, commissioning them to this ministry.
- Infusing corporate worship with songs and prayers from the world church, laments preventing worship becoming anaemic or escapist, contextual liturgy earthing the church in its own community, and testimonies celebrating signs of God at work.
- Regular conversations about finance that differentiate money spent on mission and maintenance, identify priorities, set limits on expenditure on maintenance and monitor progress towards increasing expenditure on mission.

From Institution to Movement

But even if congregations introduce such processes and become genuinely missional, this will not accomplish the paradigm shift needed for church after Christendom. We need action at the translocal level (of networks, agencies and denominations) to shift from institution to movement, following through commitments such as the *Lambeth Pastoral Letter* expressed in 1988: 'We believe that the Holy Spirit is now leading us to become a movement for mission.'

During the 1990s Anglicans and others focused on building missionary congregations. This was a reasonable starting point, but congregational action is insufficient. Indeed, excessive emphasis on church-as-congregation may hinder missional thinking and the emergence of church-as-movement. What action, rooted in missiological reflection on our post-Christendom context, might catalyse and sustain a missional movement?

Denominations can become missional movements. Policies and strategy documents that use missional language but leave institutional life unaltered are misleading, even counter-productive. An exercise of corporate imagination is required with practical outcomes subject to ongoing monitoring. Each denomination can pursue this in ways that are congruent with its history and ecclesial convictions, but radical changes are needed in self-identity, priorities, structure and ethos. For example:

- Subsuming other departments under its mission department, or abolishing the distinction between 'home mission' and 'overseas mission' and reassigning denominational staff and functions to its mission agency.

- Appointing to translocal roles people with pioneering and strategic gifts, who are mission-minded and oriented towards envisioning, risk taking and change management.
- Catalysing strategic church planting that pioneers fresh expressions of church on behalf of the denomination, offering pioneers freedom to experiment and supportive accountability.
- Introducing a parallel 'church pruning' strategy, whereby unhealthy churches that discredit the gospel and deflect resources from mission are encouraged to close.[3]
- Aiming to spend over half of denominational funds on mission, recognising this redistribution of resources will reshape the denomination. Finance is a measurable indicator of progress towards a paradigm shift.[4]
- Creating a monitoring process whereby representatives of other denominations participate regularly in conversations reviewing progress on these issues.

Training institutions can resource missional movements. The Christendom mindset pervades many theological

---

[3]   Peter Selby suggests in relation to such a congregation that 'it might be important to prevent it from extending its membership and so absorbing the energies of more and more people in activities that are not only useless but have the added disadvantage of claiming to be immensely important.' Quoted in Kenneth Leech, *Through our Long Exile* (London: Darton, Longman & Todd, 2001), 197.

[4]   Currently some denominations spend 90 per cent of their budget on the 10 per cent of the population who belong to church: Richard Thomas, *Counting People In* (London: SPCK, 2003), 144.

colleges and their influence will scupper progress unless they embrace this paradigm shift. This might mean:

- Disavowing their bias towards the pastors and teachers who dominated the Christendom era and concentrating instead on apostles, prophets and evangelists.
- Adapting their selection processes to ensure they recruit mission-oriented students with the character and skills for ministry in post-Christendom.
- Revising their curricula: not just adding mission modules or specialist courses but teaching *all* subjects from a missional perspective and training *all* students for cross-cultural mission.[5]
- Retraining graduates trained under the old paradigm, especially those moving from local to translocal roles.
- Developing partnerships with local congregations to help 'prepare [all] God's people for works of service'.
- Offering emerging churches and church leavers opportunities and resources for theological reflection.

Parachurch organisations can model missional movements. Such organisations re-energised the church in the Christendom era, with or without institutional approval, but were always regarded as subsidiary to the institutional church operating through congregations. Their contribution in recent decades has been immense. They have pioneered diverse missional initiatives, often in partnership with

---

[5] See further Mission Theological Advisory Group, *Presence and Prophecy: A Heart for Mission in Theological Education* (London: CTBI/Church House, 2002).

congregations, and have helped many potential church leavers rediscover vision and purpose.

Church after Christendom might resemble a parachurch organisation more than a congregation. In *Post-Christendom* I suggested using 'church' as a verb. 'This signals transition from institution to movement, sidesteps interminable discussions about structures and makes obsolete the ungainly and inappropriate term "parachurch" for creative and mission-oriented aspects of church.'[6] Accepting parachurch groups as authentically ecclesial might also help us embrace emerging churches that bear little resemblance to inherited congregations but are mission-oriented and unmistakeably ecclesial in ethos and function.

If congregations are struggling to become missional, can we envisage denominations and training institutions becoming and resourcing movements? Earlier chapters asked if church after Christendom would evolve or emerge, exploring this at congregational level. What signs are there at translocal level of a shift from institution to movement in inherited church?

- During the 1990s the Baptist Union attempted to recalibrate the denomination for mission. The process was demanding and time will tell how effective it has been, but Baptists are currently bucking the trend of decline. Someone from another denomination 'accompanied' the Baptist Union as a 'critical friend'.[7]
- The Assemblies of God, whose church planting strategy foundered in the mid–1990s, have embraced a new corporate vision to reshape the denomination,

---

[6] Murray, *Post-Christendom*, 308.
[7] Under the auspices of *Building Bridges of Hope:* see www.ctbi.org.uk/bbh.

re-purpose congregations and plan a new planting strategy. Their transformation process involves the curriculum of their college becoming more missional and 'resource congregations' developing as bases for church planting.

- *Mission-shaped Church* suggests that Anglicans are not only complementing the inherited parochial model with fresh expressions of church but allowing their missiology to shape their ecclesiology. Oxford diocese's *Cutting Edge* project represents substantial financial investment in emerging church in the hope of learning valuable lessons for the benefit of the wider church.

- The Salvation Army, facing prospects as bleak as any inherited denomination, in 2004 launched ALOVE, 'the Salvation Army for a new generation'. Rooted in the denomination's history and values, this movement within the institution represents an attempt to recover the Army's early missional dynamic.

Are these initiatives too little too late? Several denominations face meltdown by 2030, as continuing decline threatens their viability. Multi-directional membership transfers between churches in a post-denominational era undermine denominational stability. Are denominations, forged in modernity, inherently institutional and too cumbersome for a postmodern environment? John and Olive Drane conclude: 'At denominational level, none of our churches has really succeeded in making the paradigm shift from maintenance to mission.'[8] Can inherited denomi-

---

[8] John and Olive Drane, 'Breaking into Dynamic Ways of being Church' in *Breaking New Ground* (material prepared for the First Scottish Ecumenical Assembly, 2001), 144.

nations evolve into networks that will sustain a post-Christendom missional movement?

Networks are essential for a movement to flourish (and for the conversations chapter 4 advocated). The perspectives and experiences of emerging and inherited churches might be mutually helpful.

Some emerging churches began spontaneously and remain isolated. Many connect via informal networks, web-based communities and occasional gatherings. Others relate to denominations or mission agencies (such as Urban Expression or Cutting Edge).[9] Interactive websites[10] facilitate storytelling and theological reflection. And the role of networkers and mentors, supporting emerging churches and building links, represents a more helpful contemporary expression of 'apostolic' ministry than the high-profile role usually associated with this term. These expressions of networking can stimulate inherited denominations to develop new patterns of relating.

But the (positive and negative) experience of inherited churches can help emerging churches develop patterns of relating that will sustain them over the long haul. Loose networks, informal coalitions, relational links and other forms of 'liquid church'[11] are essential in this emerging phase but may be inadequate to sustain a post-Christendom missional movement. Any emerging infrastructure could revert to institutional mode; but without infrastructure emerging churches may simply dissipate without catalysing a missional movement. Developing post-Christendom missional networks might be another fruit of symbiosis between inherited and emerging churches.

---

[9] See www.urbanexpression.org.uk and www.oxford.anglican. org/cutting_edge/

[10] For example, www.emergingchurch.info and www.opensourcetheology.com.

[11] See Ward, *Liquid Church*.

A Sceptical Interlude

Proposing a paradigm shift from 'institution' to 'movement' as a prerequisite for post-Christendom ecclesiology provokes sceptical responses. Some assert the sociological inevitability of movements becoming institutions. All renewal movements throughout church history have followed this course, losing their missional impetus and adopting institutional characteristics in order to survive. The dissident movements introduced in *Post-Christendom* experienced this. Even the first-century Jesus movement became quite institutional well before Christendom! Christendom may be the maturing rather than subversion of the Christian movement. So why bother advocating a shift that will be temporary?

But even if this process is inevitable, we can still re-imagine church as a movement. Church history reveals the interplay of periods of institutionalisation and renewal movements. Some movements thrived for decades and sparked fresh initiatives. On the threshold of post-Christendom, even a temporary shift is worthwhile; remaining in institutional mode will be disastrous. Furthermore, there are organisational processes whereby movements can be revitalised rather than succumbing to institutionalisation.

Proposing a paradigm shift from 'maintenance' to 'mission' also invites scepticism – and, through over-familiarity with these concepts, weariness. This shift is sometimes misrepresented through unwarranted polarisation. Mission without maintenance is unsustainable. Dividing activities into static categories labelled 'maintenance' and 'mission' is simplistic.

However, caricature and polarisation aside, challenging the maintenance orientation that marginalised mission during the Christendom era is vital. Mission *is* the church's agenda; maintenance comprises crucial items on the agenda. This mission shapes the church; appropriate maintenance sustains it. Unattractive churches are ineffective in mission; non-missional churches will not survive. Rediscovering the pre-Christendom mission orientation is crucial in post-Christendom.

How we read Ephesians 4 reveals our orientation towards maintenance or mission. On the surface it contains little overtly missional. With the exception of 'evangelists' (and perhaps 'apostles'), it concentrates on building a healthy church. In Christendom, this interpretation was natural (as was the excision of evangelists, apostles and prophets). But this letter was written to participants in a marginal mission movement. Once we recognise its context, we cannot interpret its contents without reference to this. The passage is about healthy attitudes and processes, about multi-voiced and multi-gifted community, but it presupposes what is explicit elsewhere in Ephesians – that those receiving these instructions are engaged in mission.

Mission-oriented interpretation insists the 'works of service' for which the community is 'prepared' are mainly missional; the gifts each has received are for use beyond as well as within the community; and those who are being prepared, not those who do the preparing, are on the front line. This missional thrust – from the ascended Christ through the preparers to the community and out in works of service – was reversed by the Christendom paradigm, where the laity supported the clergy as they performed ecclesial and ritual 'works of service'.

This pattern persists in many churches. Faithful membership is measured in terms of meetings attended, support for church leaders and financial contributions; the 'works of service' are performed by church leaders. This is a Christendom toxin, powerfully present especially in larger churches; it is deadly and needs purging from the system. Eddie Gibbs concludes: 'to release its people for their God-assigned tasks, the large, successful church must be prepared to dismantle a great number of its centralized meetings and activities that depend upon professional clergy aided by an army of volunteers.'[12]

Despite the scepticism provoked by advocating these paradigm shifts, it is essential we explore their implications. The experience of emerging churches is mixed here: many consciously abolish institutional patterns; some allow their mission context to shape their community; others constitute themselves as missional movements; and still others renounce inherited perspectives on mission but are unsure what mission now means. James Thwaites' writings have influenced some emerging churches. He advocates a missional approach to Ephesians 4: 'the equipping of saints for works of service was for all of life, rather than primarily an equipping for local church life ... the saints' works are more important than that of the leaders.'[13]

There are signs, and counter-signs, that shifts from institution to movement and from maintenance to mission are underway. But the Christendom legacy and the lure of maintenance-oriented institutionalism will require constant vigilance if we begin to make progress. For church after Christendom, however, these shifts are essential if it is to survive.

From the Centre to the Margins

As in pre-Christendom, church after Christendom will operate on the margins. Many resist the implications of this

---

[12] Eddie Gibbs and Ian Coffey *Church Next: Quantum Changes in Christian Ministry* (Leicester: Inter-Varsity Press, 2001), 32.

[13] James Thwaites, *Renegotiating the Church Contract: The Death and Life of the 21st Century Church* (Carlisle: Paternoster, 2001), 73, 81–2.

shift. Acknowledging, indeed welcoming, the church's marginality prompts accusations of defeatism. Confidence is already low in many churches, sapped by decades of declining numbers and social influence. Elsewhere, younger movements and larger churches sustain the hope that revival will restore the church's fortunes and reputation or the illusion that nothing has really changed. This paradigm shift is unpopular and uncongenial.

But hailing as counter-evidence opinion polls that merely confirm the predictable but diminishing persistence of notional Christianity at the end of Christendom, pointing to burgeoning churches as if these are typical, and investing enormous hopes in mission strategies still rooted in Christendom assumptions – these increasingly desperate ploys offer no credible grounds for avoiding the conclusion that churches are becoming ever more marginal in Western societies.

Acknowledging this is a matter of honesty, not defeatism. Responding to the challenge of post-Christendom without accepting this marginality is counter-productive. We are not starting at the right point, so our assumptions will be skewed and our expectations unrealistic. Furthermore, our self-image, attitudes, tone of voice and ways of relating will further damage the already tarnished reputation of an institution associated with a fading culture characterised by oppression, moralism and hypocrisy.

Welcoming this is a matter of judgement, not despair. The end of Christendom marks the collapse of a determined but ultimately futile attempt to impose Christianity rather than inviting people to follow Jesus. The fourth-century decision to transfer from the margins to the centre in one enormous leap for power resulted in coercive but nominal Christianity. It also deflected a missional movement that had, from the margins, made extraordinary progress during the past three centuries and might have permeated and transformed the Empire from the grass roots. Subversive but effective 'mustard seed' and 'yeast-in-the-dough' strategies[14] gave way to top-down religion. The marginality of post-Christendom churches holds out the enticing prospect of recovering the power and appeal of subversive Christianity and getting the missional movement back on track.

Identifying the centre

If Christianity is no longer at the centre, what is? Identifying the metanarrative that dominates post-Christendom is crucial if we would tell another story in language and images that engage with contemporary culture. But there is disagreement about this.

During the past half-century proponents of the 'secularisation thesis' have concluded post-Christendom will be constituted by *secularity*. Although they debate the process, its time frame and the influence and inter-relationship of causal factors, proponents agree that the end of Christendom means transition to a culture dominated by secular values. This does not preclude the persistence of Christianity and other religions (old and new) on the margins, but religious ideas and values will no longer shape Western culture.

Over the past twenty-five years others have challenged the accuracy and adequacy of this thesis. Few doubt the influence of secularity, but many (including some formerly committed to the secularisation paradigm) detect a counter-trend of 'desecularisation' and suggest *spirituality* – in multiple forms – will thrive in post-Christendom. They note, for example:

---

[14] Matthew 13:31–33.

- Evidence from polls and surveys of widespread enthusiasm for and diffuse experiences of spirituality.
- A burgeoning market in spirituality and spiritual elements in popular culture (films, magazines, songs, games, etc.).
- Testimony from youth workers of interest among young people in various forms of spirituality.
- The influence of New Age spirituality, paganism and Eastern religions.

Many emerging churches have bought unreservedly into this prognosis, bewailing the secularity of inherited churches and developing styles of worship and community they hope can connect with this resurgent spirituality. They are under no illusions that this spirituality is essentially Christian, but they regard spirituality as the focus for mission in postmodernity. Some inherited churches share this perception and are repenting of secular values they have imbibed.

But how prevalent is this interest in spirituality, how significant is it and how long will it last? Steve Bruce, an unrepentant advocate of the secularisation thesis, doubts the evidence for spiritual resurgence. In *God is Dead* he systematically deconstructs the case for spirituality returning to the cultural centre, debunking suggestions that the evidence amounts to more than ephemeral phenomena around the fringes of a secular culture. He dismisses interpretations of surveys as 'unreasonably optimistic' attempts to assert the persistence of Christian beliefs, regards the New Age movement as failed and fading,[15] and insists innocuous and

---

[15] 'Even the most generous estimates of the New Age are unlikely to have the new spiritual seekers filling the space left by the decline of just one denomination.' Bruce, *God is Dead*, 81.

undemanding Westernised versions of Eastern religions will have little lasting impact.

Bruce concludes there is 'considerable and consistent evidence that conventional religious beliefs are declining in popularity' and 'there is no sign of any new religious phenomenon to fill the space. Britain is indeed becoming secular.'[16] Callum Brown concurs:

> the rise of non-Christian religions and quasi-religions (including New Religions and New Age movements) did not, have not and will not fill the void of religiosity left by the decline of Christianity ... what Britain has experienced since 1963 is "genuine" secularisation.[17]

Other researchers and sociologists interpret the evidence differently, especially those who believe human beings are innately and incorrigibly religious and that secularity is an inadequate long-term basis for society.[18] Many Christians who agree with this hope the resurgent interest in spirituality they detect, despite the scepticism of Brown and Bruce, offers fresh opportunities for mission if we can transform the church to engage with a more spiritual culture.

---

[16] Bruce, *God is Dead*, 197, 60.

[17] Callum Brown, 'The secularisation debate: what the 1960s have done to the study of religious history', in Hugh McLeod and Werner Ustorf (eds.), *The Decline of Christendom in Western Europe, 1750–2000* (Cambridge: Cambridge University Press, 2003), 35.

[18] For example, Grace Davie, *Religion in Britain since 1945: Believing without Belonging* (Oxford: Blackwell, 1994); Rodney Stark and William Bainbridge, *A Theory of Religion* (New York: Peter Lang, 1987). To compare these approaches, see Jeffrey Cox, 'Master narratives of long-term religious change' in McLeod and Ustorf, *Decline*, 201–17.

But the scepticism of those who defend the secularisation thesis should make us wary of misinterpreting our context and misconstruing our response. Defining the centre of our culture in terms of spirituality and shaping our churches and mission strategies in light of this definition may be unwise.

- Is the interest in spirituality mainly confined to white middle-class Westerners? Bruce suggests this.[19] If so, our reshaped churches and mission strategies will reach only one section of society – the section we always prioritise.
- Is the interest in spirituality only temporary? Those classified as Generation X (born between 1961 and 1977) may exhibit hunger for spiritual experience, but Generation Y (born since 1977) may be less interested. In a recent research project 'spirituality barely gets a mention' from under twenties. This challenges the 'false assumption that young people have a latent spirituality simply waiting to be activated'.[20]
- Is contemporary spirituality a designer accessory that does not engage people at depth or impact their core beliefs, values and priorities? If so, it may not be a stepping stone towards Christian faith but inoculation against it.
- Is contemporary spirituality instinctively, and often explicitly, post-Christian or anti-Christian? If so, hopes that spirituality may be a conduit into Christian faith and church may be unfounded.
- Is post-Christian spirituality fulfilling the role allotted to Christianity since the Enlightenment –

[19] Bruce, *God is Dead*, 88–9.
[20] Booker and Ireland, *Evangelism*, 173.

satisfying private spiritual needs without challenging secular values at the core of society? If so, mission in post-Christendom may require renewed engagement with secularism – perhaps as our main priority.

None of this implies post-Christendom churches should miss opportunities to urge those interested in spirituality to explore Christianity. Nor should we refrain from planting churches configured for this context, or duck the challenge of reorienting inherited churches more profoundly warped by secularisation than we have realised. But we will beware identifying spirituality as the centre of post-Christendom society and developing ecclesial or missional responses shaped exclusively by this aspect of culture. This is a worrying imbalance in some emerging churches, a consequence of over-emphasising or misinterpreting the shift from modernity to postmodernity.

Post-Christendom implies that Christian beliefs and values are no longer accepted as the metanarrative of Western culture. The prevalence of 'post' words in analyses of our culture suggests an alternative metanarrative is not yet apparent. Our society is diverse and requires diverse ecclesial and missional responses. 'Spiritual searchers' is one of seven categories John Drane identifies in answer to the question 'whom are we trying to reach?' Others are the desperate poor, hedonists, traditionalists, corporate achievers, secularists and the apathetic.[21] The challenge is to find appropriate ways of incarnating the gospel among all of these groups. The creativity and courage of some emerging churches as they focus on marginalised subcultures is a hopeful sign. This challenge is not insuperable. But a full-orbed response will need the combined efforts – and mutual support – of inherited and emerging churches. An

---

[21] Drane, *McDonaldization*, 55–84.

urgent and ongoing issue is identifying the people our churches and strategies are neglecting.

Is there, then, no centre in contemporary culture? This is a common postmodern view, which some missiologists echo, interpreting Western society as a jumble of fragments without a definable centre or metanarrative. If this is so, the discussion in this section is misleading: in a decentred culture, there are no margins.

But there are serious problems with this analysis (which sounds suspiciously like a hidden, and thus dangerous, metanarrative):

- It overplays discontinuity between inherited and emerging culture. There are radical differences between modernity and postmodernity, but (as terms like 'late-modernity', 'hyper-modernity' and 'liquid modernity' indicate) there is also continuity and reinforcement. Economism, consumerism, individualism, militarism, technological dependency, globalisation and other forces shaping our culture flourished in modernity and persist in postmodernity.[22]
- It ignores power dynamics in society, whereby those with power and wealth dominate and marginalise others. Rejecting ideas of centre and margins plays into their hands. The Christendom church colluded with the power-brokers at the centre; in post-Christendom we dare not to collude with an analysis that benefits the powerful and continues to marginalise others.

---

[22] Walter Brueggemann suggests 'military consumerism' is the true metanarrative in contemporary Western society. See his *Theology of the Old Testament: Testimony, Dispute, Advocacy* (Minneapolis: Fortress, 1997), 718, and elsewhere.

Mission from the margins

Becoming again a marginal mission movement means rejecting many attitudes and assumptions inherited from Christendom. The invitation is to return to our roots and recapture the subversive pre-Christendom dynamism that turned the world upside down from the margins.[23] Repositioning our churches – theologically, attitudinally and strategically – on the margins is essential. Resisting marginality will jeopardise our capacity to regroup and discover fresh ways of engaging with post-Christendom society.

Leonard Sweet uses 'the sporting analogy of "playing away" to describe the current missionary condition of the post-Constantinian church'[24] – an evocative metaphor for mission from the margins. We are not 'at home' as we were in Christendom; we must adjust our attitudes, strategy and expectations. What might this mean?

- *Assuming less knowledge of Christianity*. Most process evangelism courses assume greater familiarity with Christian terminology and concepts than we can expect as memories of Christendom fade. Hugh McLeod warns: 'The decline of Christendom has meant that Christianity has been gradually losing its status as a lingua franca, and has tended to become a local language used by those who are professing Christians, but not understood by others.'[25]

---

[23] But post-Christendom is not pre-Christendom revisited. We can disavow Christendom but cannot disown its chequered history, which contains both wonderful resources and damaging legacies.

[24] Leonard Sweet, *Quantum Spirituality: A Postmodern Apologetic* (Dayton: Spirit Venture Ministries, 1994), 194.

[25] McLeod and Ustorf, *Decline*, 11.

- *Anticipating longer journeys towards faith.* Most process evangelism courses move quickly towards assumptions that participants have embraced Christian faith and now need to be discipled. This is unsurprising since some evolved from courses written for new Christians, but in post-Christendom evangelism and discipling will both take longer. Evangelism will start further back and move more slowly; induction will continue much further. Patience is essential for mission and community-building after Christendom.
- *Allowing others to set the agenda.* Most process evangelism courses set the agenda for discussion. They may allow participants to ask other questions, but organisers assume they know which issues are most important and so refocus conversations on these. Such imposition demands less of the organisers but is inappropriate if we are 'playing away'. Engaging with the agendas of others and discovering gospel connections is more authentic.

Just as some emerging churches may be transitional, so current process evangelism courses may be stepping stones from outdated approaches to truly post-Christendom strategies. *Alpha* and similar initiatives encourage belonging before believing, rely on friendships rather than events, combine apologetics and spiritual encounter and make use of dialogue and small groups. These elements have been effective in recent years and remain essential. But courses that have engaged mainly with the semi-churched and de-churched must be radically reconfigured to connect with the pre-churched and anti-churched in post-Christendom.

Moreover, tinkering with invitational strategies is inadequate. Eddie Gibbs insists: 'when the church finds itself marginalized and existing as just one piece in a complex

social kaleidoscope in which the pieces are constantly
realigning ... the church must not only be inviting but infiltrating.'[26] Process evangelism and seeker-sensitive events
represent advances on old-style evangelistic events or guest
services, but they are still invitational rather than
incarnational. The demise of Christendom requires a
missional rather than *evangelistic* strategy.[27]

Although both 'gathered' and 'dispersed' forms of mission will still be needed, we will prioritise dispersed
strategies.[28] Mission from the margins means 'playing
away', or engaging with people in their own context –
which is often, in a networked society, not where they live
but where they work or relax. Neighbourhood evangelism
will be appropriate only in certain areas. Elsewhere,
churches will concentrate on equipping their members to
live authentic and attractive Christian lives and to share
their faith 'away from home'. Some emerging churches
exemplify this incarnational approach – which inherited
church strategists have also recommended. Well-known
examples are Raymond Fung's 'Isaiah Agenda' and Ann
Morisy's work on 'community ministry.[29]

This approach to mission deliberately blurs the boundaries between evangelism and social action.
Twentieth-century debates about these aspects of mission
presupposed that a powerful church might abuse those for
whom it provided practical support by imposing conditions

---

[26] Gibbs and Coffey, *Church*, 167.
[27] See Booker and Ireland, *Evangelism*, 161–3.
[28] Warren, *Signs of Life*, 71.
[29] Raymond Fung, *The Isaiah Agenda* (Geneva: WCC, 1992);
Ann Morisy, *Beyond the Good Samaritan: Community Ministry
and Mission* (London: Mowbray, 1997). An emerging church
version of this approach – 'proximity spaces' – features in Frost
and Hirsch, *Shaping*.

on its largesse or practising covert evangelism. Post-Christendom churches will not be immune to this temptation, but three factors offer protection: they will be relatively powerless; they will more likely be partners than patrons; and most initiatives will foster empowerment, not dependency. This may liberate churches to engage in holistic, sensitive and unapologetic contextual mission.

Morisy, defining the end of Christendom as an 'adaptive zone', has recently offered a 'new approach to Christian mission' embracing three elements: foundational, explicit and vocational domains. The *explicit* domain, in which people hear the story of Jesus, remains crucial but requires prior activity in other domains. The *foundational* domain involves encouraging people to 'build their confidence in the intimations they have of an enduring reality and the non-material aspects of life'.[30] In this domain our task is to help people consider the *possibility* of God and embark on or pursue a spiritual quest. Morisy concludes: 'the foundational domain is a new field for evangelism that has come into being because of the ending of a Christendom culture.'[31]

This approach starts further back than process evangelism courses. It presupposes a more pervasive influence of secularisation than some concede. For people already interested in spirituality, work in the foundational domain is also necessary (since few connect spirituality with Christianity and even fewer with church), but it will take a different shape. In either context, starting further back means patiently sowing seeds without expecting an imminent harvest.

Post-Christendom presented two snapshots of people whose complete unfamiliarity with the story of Jesus and

---

[30] Morisy, *Journeying*, 151–2.
[31] Morisy, *Journeying*, 175.

the church provoked great curiosity.[32] Such snapshots are increasingly common. A teenager was fascinated by the 'magic square' on Gaudi's Sagrada Familia Cathedral in Barcelona, in which many numerical combinations add up to 33. 'Why 33?' she asked. 'Because Jesus died at that age.' 'That was young – what did he die of?' Walking into the cathedral she continued, 'Who's that woman and why does she always have a baby?'

The *vocational* domain, Morisy writes, 'is about encouraging and enabling people to express discipleship, regardless of whether they are Christian'.[33] She gives examples of various forms of community ministry that enable Christians and others to partner together in the struggle for justice and transformation of individuals and communities. In the process, everyone reflects on their beliefs and priorities. This is a new slant on the relationship between belonging, believing and behaving: behaving may stimulate believing and belonging.[34]

This approach is an alternative to the popular but flawed 'need-oriented evangelism', which reinforces the Christendom dependency model and presents an anaemic version of the gospel of the kingdom.[35] And it removes power dynamics from the equation, as Christians become fellow strugglers, rather than sources of superior knowledge or virtue. This is a helpful strategy for marginal mission communities.

---

[32] Murray, *Post-Christendom*, 1.

[33] Morisy, *Journeying*, 218.

[34] Although not entirely new, as early church catechists also expected behavioural change to induct people into new ways of thinking and believing.

[35] 'Playing away' and 'allowing others to set the agenda' does not require collusion with dependency or a therapeutic culture.

Starting further back

This section has advocated 'starting further back' than was necessary in Christendom, or even in the present transitional period. But mission in post-Christendom actually starts further back than mission in pre-Christendom! Then the church had no heritage. In post-Christendom its legacy is ambivalent and its reputation sullied. Congregations may transcend this and be well regarded in their communities, but the church's image constitutes a major stumbling block to its mission. Its language, symbols and history may have negative connotations.[36] As the de-churched and semi-churched diminish, post-Christendom churches must engage creatively, sensitively and courageously with the pre-churched and anti-churched. Many of the latter are not opposed to Christianity but to its expression through imperialistic Christendom.

Mission from the margins, therefore, will include humility, contrition, repentance and honest acknowledgment that the church has not consistently incarnated the gospel. Such attitudes are not readily associated with Christendom. But there have been signs recently of willingness to face such issues, including 'reconciliation walks' to express repentance for the medieval Crusades and confession that the church has tolerated and covered up various kinds of abuse.

Less apparent is any link between confession and evangelism, such as is evident in Cornelius' house, as Peter repents of his ethnocentrism before inviting the household to receive God's forgiveness.[37] Generally, those who run process evangelism courses assume their task is to help others embrace perspectives they already have, rather than

---

[36] Cf. the discussion of the cross in Murray, *Post-Christendom*, 92–4.
[37] Acts 10:34.

engaging in genuine dialogue through which all can learn and grow. Acknowledging limited understanding, capacity to be wrong and 'solidarity in sinfulness'[38] transforms the attitudes with which we evangelise. The tone of voice post-Christendom churches adopt will be as critical as the content of their message.

Starting further back also means reflecting, not just on evangelistic strategies, but on the gospel. A disappointing aspect of many emerging churches, noted in chapter 3, is their theological conservatism: their readiness to explore the implications of cultural changes for the church is rarely matched by eagerness to re-examine the nature of the gospel. Contextualisation may not touch this apparently sacrosanct area of theology. But the gospel cannot be detached from the cultural context if it is to be 'good news'; we must re-translate the story of Jesus into every subculture of a plural society like post-Christendom. Holding in creative tension *faithfulness* to our founding story and *flexibility* in how we tell this story, using language and images that resonate with our context, has been the challenge whenever the church operates as a marginal mission movement.

When the church becomes a powerful institution, a particular way of telling the story solidifies and attains normative status, marginalising alternatives. It can also function as a control mechanism, enhancing the church's status. In Christendom, the story was told using images of penal substitution, forensic justification and everlasting torment. The Christendom gospel addressed the issues of *guilt* and *life after death*, offering forgiveness and eternal life, dispensed by the church as Christ's representative. It marginalised aspects of the story that might be socially disruptive: good news to the poor, the kingdom of justice and

---

[38] Morisy, *Journeying*, 176.

peace, the hope for a new earth. This version of the gospel connected with the concerns of many people, but these concerns were shaped by Christendom values, priorities and assumptions.

In post-Christendom, a culture less concerned about guilt and more interested in life before death than afterwards, this telling of the story is less helpful. Images rooted in feudalism, legal processes and retributive violence are anachronistic and unattractive. Marginal churches can reassess this version of the gospel and recover marginalised or distorted aspects of the story. The Christendom legacy is oppressive, with accusations of unorthodoxy awaiting any who dare challenge the inherited version. Perhaps this is why many emerging churches seem reluctant to embark on this. But marginal mission movements can be more sensitive to their context, more courageous in re-translating the story and more discerning about the resonance and dissonance between this story and their cultural setting. The witness of dissident movements through the centuries and of missionaries in other cultures confirms this.[39]

The dissident tradition emphasises one particular dimension of the gospel distorted by Christendom: it is good news to the poor. Marginal post-Christendom churches may rediscover a radical gospel that subverts condescending 'need-oriented evangelism' (that leaves unchallenged an unjust status quo) and reconnects evangelism with social justice. If the gospel is truly good news to the poor, we have not been preaching the gospel, for the rich and powerful have not found it disturbing and the poor have not found it liberating.

While churches were associated with power and wealth it was difficult to detect this problem – 'power has been the

---

[39] A modern classic is Vincent Donovan, *Christianity Rediscovered* (London: SCM, 2001).

poison that has prevented the institutional Church from understanding the gospel'[40] – but the powerlessness of marginal churches offers hope. Those hearing the gospel in post-Christendom will be starting further back: but those *sharing* the gospel must also start further back. This challenge – to rediscover the 'gospel of the kingdom' and tell the story in fresh ways – is not only for inherited churches but for emerging churches, few of which live among the poor and powerless.

The problem of evangelism

Mission does not comprise only evangelism. There are other dimensions to becoming a marginal mission movement, many of which other books in the *After Christendom* series will address. But evangelism is especially problematic. Despite lessons learned during the Decade of Evangelism, evangelism remains unpopular (in practice, if not in theory) in inherited churches. Robert Warren concedes: 'while getting evangelism onto the agenda of the Church, the Decade has not yet got the good news onto the lips of church members in any great measure.'[41] Many church leavers express distaste for the ways churches practise evangelism. Some emerging churches avoid evangelism altogether.

And yet:

- Without evangelism there will be no church after Christendom, nor any way of sustaining other dimensions of mission.
- Churches (inherited and emerging) that do not evangelise but are parasitic on churches that do eventually find recruits drying up.

---

[40] Morisy, *Journeying*, 233.
[41] Warren, *Signs*, 49.

- Christianity is an evangelistic faith and most Christians deep down want to share their faith, even if they hate the thought of 'evangelism'.
- Despite language, images, attitudes and processes that contravene everything this section has advocated, evangelising churches continue to attract people.
- Some church leavers, no longer obliged to link evangelism with invitations to church, experience unexpected freedom in sharing their faith.
- The recent creative outburst that has sparked a plethora of emerging churches is paralleled by the creativity that has produced a remarkable range of fresh approaches to evangelism.[42]

Rehabilitating, rather than abandoning, evangelism and discovering authentic ways of sharing faith is essential for post-Christendom churches.[43] Purging the Christendom toxins needs to be followed by creative and courageous action to envision and equip churches for evangelistic 'works of service', using their diverse gifts. This alone will not transform the church into a marginal mission movement, but this transformation cannot be accomplished without it.

---

[42] See Booker and Ireland, *Evangelism*, passim.
[43] See further Murray, *Post-Christendom*, 225–32.

6

Church After Christendom: Community

The shift from maintenance to mission does not imply disregard for internal church dynamics. Neglecting the health and inner life of missional communities undermines the confidence of those who are sharing faith with their friends, disenchants any who begin to belong before they believe and accelerates the exodus of leavers. Building healthy, honest and harmonious communities is a prerequisite for effective mission.[1]

Healthy Churches

In the 1980s, many asked how churches could *grow* and welcomed programmes and strategies that promised to deliver this. Some insisted growth was multidimensional, but numerical growth, more easily measured than other dimensions, was primary. In the 1990s, many asked how churches could *multiply*; church planting and cell church offered processes designed for reproduction. Some insisted that the kinds of churches planted mattered more than the number, but the momentum generated by numerical targets inhibited discussion.

---

[1] This chapter focuses on issues the post-Christendom lens reveals unusually clearly.

In the 2000s, some are asking how churches can *survive*. Growth and multiplication remain desirable, but issues marginalised during the 1980s and 1990s are back on the agenda. What kinds of churches do we need? What other dimensions of growth are crucial? Inherited and emerging churches are asking these questions.

Many emerging churches are committed to good relationships, healthy processes and empowering structures. Some are completely uninterested in numerical growth; most are more interested in quality than quantity. There is widespread suspicion that 'size matters' and that small-scale churches may be healthier than large ones and less prone to impersonal organisation, power politics and institutional inertia. Some are finding, however, that size alone is no guarantee. Healthy processes must be learned.

Many inherited churches have prioritised quality – although decline and depressing projections of future viability may challenge their stance. Some question whether this quality/quantity dichotomy is useful, believing growth in quality stimulates numerical growth. Others are reluctant to dispense with this dichotomy: growth in quantity and quality do not always go together. Those who listen at the back door of their churches know that leavers perceive many churches as unhealthy or dysfunctional communities.

Church health, then, must be high on the agenda of post-Christendom churches. How can we nurture the attitudes and interpersonal skills Ephesians 4 lists (love, humility, gentleness, truthfulness, patience)? This is neither a wish-list nor a set of sticks with which to beat each other. Healthy churches, whether evolving from inherited churches or emerging afresh, do not just happen. Churches comprise 'recovering sinners', who bruise, compete with, misunderstand, neglect and disappoint each other. Endorsing Ephesians 4 and expressing fine intentions are insufficient. We need processes and practices that challenge unhealthy attitudes and behaviour, train our reflexes and build community.

From growth to health

A shift from 'growth' to 'health' is already apparent in some church circles. Anglican Church Planting Initiatives, for example, has renamed its *Planting for Growth* course *Planting Healthy Churches*. In 2003, Healthy Church UK replaced the British Church Growth Association. It promotes Natural Church Development (NCD). This assesses church health against eight 'quality characteristics': empowering leadership, gift-orientated lay ministry, passionate spirituality, functional structures, inspiring worship services, holistic small groups, need-orientated evangelism and loving relationships.[2]

Robert Warren, who wrote extensively on mission in the 1990s,[3] has also turned his attention to church health. Building critically on the NCD approach, he field-tested his own quality characteristics under Springboard's 'Healthy Churches' initiative. In *The Healthy Churches' Handbook* he suggests a healthy church is energised by faith, has an outward-looking focus, seeks to find out what God wants, faces the cost of change and growth, operates as a community, makes room for all, and does a few things and does them well.[4]

This shift of emphasis is significant and the analyses and tools offered are helpful. But are they adequate for post-Christendom churches? NCD, although very popular

---

[2] See www.ncd-international.org. For an assessment, see Booker and Ireland, *Evangelism*, 122–38.

[3] See previous chapters, especially 2 and 5.

[4] Robert Warren, *The Healthy Churches' Handbook* (London: Church House, 2004).

and promoted as applicable to any situation, may be insufficiently radical. Its assumptions about mission, evangelism, the focus of church activities and the nature of leadership seem rooted in a Christendom mindset. This is an ecclesiocentric church growth tool for enlarging inherited churches. It pays little attention to contextual factors. What if post-Christendom needs different kinds of churches that do not fit the template? What if healthy churches in an exilic context do not grow? And the definition of health with which this programme works is narrow by comparison with the biblical agenda.[5]

Furthermore, although these programmes measure church health and suggest practical steps to improve this, they do not probe deeply into the dysfunctionality and systemic sickness of many churches. They do not investigate the ingrained Christendom legacy or its impact on church culture over many generations. Nor do they factor in the low esteem in which many churches are held. They address neither the anguish of church leavers nor the bemusement of people attracted to Jesus but repelled by the church. At best, these programmes may help relatively healthy churches become more attractive to people like those they already attract. At worst, they may be guilty of conspiring to 'dress the wound of my people as though it were not serious'.[6] For inherited churches to evolve into healthy post-Christendom churches, something more radical is needed.

Are emerging churches healthy?

Are there fresh perspectives or resources in emerging churches for building healthy churches? Many offer a more

---

[5] See further the critique of NCD and Warren in Croft, *Transforming*, 60–2.
[6] Jeremiah 6:14 and 8:11.

trenchant critique of inherited church culture than most 'church health' programmes. Some have developed alternative processes in relation to biblical interpretation, corporate worship, leadership, decision making, accountability and change management. These are partly intuitions, partly reactions to experiences in inherited churches, partly the consequence of different priorities or structures, and partly the outcome of theological reflection on church and culture.

But many emerging churches also struggle to build healthy communities. Inhibiting factors include: idealistic reluctance to establish guidelines or structures; aversion to leadership that leaves them open to the forces of chaos or co-option; unresolved angst brought by church leavers; and overemphasis on changing the shape of church rather than its ethos. Many emerging churches are sensitive to the unhealthy influences of modernity on inherited churches and are eager to develop postmodern approaches to community, but some are insufficiently critical of unhealthy tendencies in postmodern culture. Moreover, most are poorly sensitised to the toxic influence of Christendom.

Inherited and emerging churches need each other. The penetrating critique and fresh perspectives of some emerging churches can help inherited churches re-examine their own systems, structures and processes. Emerging churches, if they can look beyond aspects of inherited church they find alienating, can learn much from the checks and balances, principles and practices that have developed over many years. A symbiotic approach to building healthy communities could be fruitful.

The Christendom toxins

How does the Christendom legacy hinder healthy churches emerging or evolving? We need to revisit issues

Post-Christendom identified in light of the Ephesians 4 model of a healthy church – one in which all members of the body participate, discern together what is helpful or harmful for the community and speak truth to each other in love.

A systemic issue is disempowerment of the laity by clerical dominance.[7] For centuries most Christians were not allowed to take initiatives on ecclesial matters or participate in shaping the church as a community. Their responsibilities were regularly to attend services, where they were either passive spectators or confined to prescribed responses, and to support the clergy. They were not responsible for discerning the Spirit's guidance, nurturing the church's community life, shaping its worship or developing missional strategies.

The churches, therefore, provided no training for lay people to exercise such responsibilities. Indeed, in an officially Christian society, initiation processes were minimal. Everyone was expected to know the Christian story, imbibe what to believe through a combination of liturgy, sermons and symbols and learn how to behave through a combination of pastoral admonition, custom and the approval or disapproval of the community. The culture, value system, behavioural expectations and quality of interpersonal relationships in the church were little different from other spheres of society. Inculcating principles and practices that could build healthy congregations seemed unnecessary.

Nor did churches effectively monitor their own health. Church discipline, when applied at all, dealt only with gross and outrageous behaviour or with heresy. Exercised by powerful clerical leaders, often backed by state authority, it lacked pastoral sensitivity and was often oppressive, brutal or even lethal. But this was not applied to the myriad behaviours that produced dysfunctional and unhealthy churches.

---

[7] See further Murray, *Post-Christendom*, 261–4.

Damaging attitudes, debilitating practices and broken relationships not only disrupted many churches and undermined their ministry but bequeathed a bitter legacy of unresolved disputes and sub-Christian behaviour that infected future generations.

The emergence of new denominations in late Christendom, in which members were expected to play more active roles, offered fresh opportunities. Most retained the clergy/laity distinction, but members were invited to help shape corporate worship, share in pastoral and missional responsibilities and discern the Spirit's guidance by participating in members' meetings. Many Anglican and Catholic churches now also encourage 'lay' participation, although there are still many passive and dependent congregations (and these are not unknown in other denominations and new church networks, whatever the ecclesial theory!). Some emerging churches have abandoned clericalism and are more radical in their inclusion of all as community shapers.

But enhanced participation does not automatically produce healthy churches. Indeed, increased responsibility and greater freedom to shape a community may be dangerous or even disastrous. Churches that encourage greater congregational participation have been slow to recognise the need for training and disciplinary processes. Without these, the Christendom toxins are not flushed out and these younger churches experience the damaging attitudes, debilitating practices and broken relationships that made older churches unhealthy.

This is evident from the love/hate relationship many churches have with members' meetings. They defend passionately the right and responsibility of church members to discern the Spirit's guidance together and take corporate decisions about the life and mission of the church. But their experience is often disappointing: attendance is poor, expectations are low, tempers are frayed, discussion is sterile or unfocused and safety-first decisions masquerade as the church discerning the Spirit's guidance.

Dissident groups in earlier centuries also encouraged members to participate actively and shape their communities. Because they did not accept Christendom assumptions about believing and behaving, they inducted new members into the values, beliefs and practices of their churches. Their communities were flawed and not always as healthy as they wished, but they exercised church discipline in ways that were more congruent with New Testament teaching. Their testimony to post-Christendom churches is that constructive and healthy participation necessitates training and disciplinary processes to flush out the Christendom toxins.

Building healthy churches

This raises again the issue of induction. Induction into post-Christendom churches will require more than most introductory courses offer. Those who join churches will increasingly be pre-churched rather than de-churched and will be starting further back. Many will be biblically, doctrinally and ritually illiterate and need thorough induction into the biblical story, Christian beliefs and values, spirituality and discipleship in an alien culture.

But newcomers will also need to learn how to participate in the community to which they now belong. Richter and Francis conclude: 'Any church that wants to hold on to its members must take its community-building vocation seriously.'[8] They will need to imbibe its ethos and core values and learn skills for healthy interaction.

Building healthy churches requires preventative as well as remedial action. Assessing churches' health in order to repair damage and improve their performance will always be necessary, but more can be done to prevent damage and

[8] Richter and Francis, *Gone*, 162.

nurture healthier churches. The Baptist Union of Victoria, in Australia, has produced an outstanding resource, *Fit4Life*. Its leadership team, weary of merely offering remedial help to dysfunctional churches, decided to concentrate on preventative action to develop healthier churches that would need less intervention. *Fit4Life* is a challenging but accessible process.[9] It explores issues that often cause churches to become unhealthy and offers training in:

- Self-awareness.
- Healthy communication.
- Handling differences in healthy ways.
- Healthy decision making.
- Clarifying role expectations.

It ends by encouraging churches to 'covenant for health', inviting church members to commit themselves to speak and act in ways that build up the body of Christ.

Post-Christendom churches cannot assume their members are skilled in such practices or subscribe to their underlying values. Adversarial political debate, manipulative group dynamics, conflict avoidance, insensitivity to others in discussion and similar community-threatening behaviours are prevalent in Western culture. The Christendom legacy often reinforces such practices and offers few alternatives. Empowering people to participate, encouraging open discussion and endorsing the Ephesians 4 vision of a multi-gifted community where 'each part does its work' (v. 16) is not enough. Training is needed for members' meetings to fulfil their potential, alt.worship events to reflect the contributions of all who plan them and cell churches to develop beyond revamped home groups.

---

[9] Available in Britain via the Anabaptist Network (www.anabaptistnetwork.com).

Induction courses cannot guarantee the emergence or evolution of healthy churches. But for emerging churches, especially, they offer opportunities to ensure everyone is committed to shared values and good processes. Reminders of these values and how the community has chosen to conduct itself can be built into its ongoing life. Perhaps being 'values-shaped' is more essential than being 'purpose-driven'.

But what about churches – inherited or emerging – that do not have such an induction process? *Fit4Life* can also operate in remedial mode (in the same way that churches use *Alpha* with existing members). Another resource is Bridge Builders, based at the London Mennonite Centre, which teaches churches how to handle conflict creatively rather than destructively.[10] It is essential, however, that there is widespread support for this. People must understand why it is important and commit themselves to learn the relational skills involved. Treating this process as just another programme and expecting quick-fix outcomes will not result in healthier churches.

Honest Churches

This same precondition applies to another remedial process – what Anabaptists called 'the rule of Christ', what Ephesians 4 means by 'speaking the truth in love', but what has historically been designated 'church discipline'.

Church discipline

There are many reasons to give a wide berth to something that sounds institutional, threatening, legalistic and punitive:

---

[10] See www.menno.org.uk/BB/.

- Western culture is liberal and tolerant – of everything except intolerance. Church discipline offends this notion of tolerance and the related individualism within our society.
- People already perceive many churches as moralistic and judgmental. Emerging and inherited churches want to be hospitable, accepting and open to all. Church discipline seems to point in the opposite direction.
- Many people have had bad experiences of church discipline or have heard stories of this process being abused or mishandled and causing enormous pain, damaging rather than building-up the church.
- The complex relationship between believing, behaving and belonging in post-Christendom poses questions about how church discipline might operate.
- Church discipline is not easy. Speaking the truth in love involves confrontation. It requires courage and risks rejection.
- Church discipline is hard to apply in a context of consumer choice, when people can avoid issues by decamping to another church.
- Church discipline is counter-intuitive in a context of declining numbers. The idea of possibly reducing them further by exercising discipline is unattractive.

Instinctively, or conscious of such factors, many react strongly against the notion of church discipline. Others have never seriously considered it, because they have not belonged to churches where this was practised and training courses rarely address the subject.

But there are several incentives to re-examine this much-maligned practice:

- The Gospels only place 'church' on Jesus' lips twice. In Matthew 16:18 Jesus promises to build a church the gates of Hades cannot withstand; in Matthew 18:15–17 he prescribes a process of loving confrontation through which this church can be sustained.
- Guidelines for and examples of church discipline feature in every strand of New Testament teaching.
- Churches are imperfect communities of would-be disciples who go astray and need restoration.[11]
- Most churches sooner or later encounter situations where loving confrontation is essential. If this is fudged, individuals and the church suffer serious damage.
- Churches that attempt to exercise church discipline in a crisis without having first taught the principles and established good processes risk chaos.
- Many church leavers cite their church's mishandling of ethical and relational issues as reasons for leaving.
- Inadequate accountability has damaged some emerging churches.[12] Others are searching for alternatives to the control mechanisms they perceive in inherited churches. New monastic communities rework ancient practices.
- In the strange new world of post-Christendom we need each other's help and support to live faithfully and distinctively.
- Churches that avoid loving confrontation become dysfunctional, dishonest and missionally ineffective.

---

[11] See Matthew 18:12–14.
[12] Most seriously, and notoriously, the pioneering Nine O'Clock Service in Sheffield.

The Christendom legacy combines neglect and abuse. Distorted expressions of church discipline include the mutual anathemas of fourth- and fifth-century church councils and the horrors of the Inquisition,[13] so it is hardly surprising the practice is unpopular. But the dissident tradition (Waldensians, Anabaptists and others) offers an alternative, though flawed, historical paradigm of 'loving confrontation',[14] suggesting we can purge the Christendom toxins and recover this community-building process.

If your brother or sister sins against you

Good intentions, shared values and effective induction courses are insufficient to sustain healthy churches. Emerging churches can heed the experience of inherited churches: things go wrong, people behave badly and unresolved issues rankle. Inherited and emerging churches reluctant to practise loving confrontation might weigh the reports of church leavers: several left because churches failed to deal responsibly with power struggles, backbiting, immature behaviour, moral lapses or broken relationships.

Jesus tells us we should lovingly confront brothers or sisters who sin against us.[15] The New Testament identifies four purposes: to restore them to fellowship with Christ and the community; to maintain a distinctive Christian ethos within the church; to deflect God's judgement; and to deter unfaithfulness.[16] Post-Christendom churches, if they would be honest and healthy, dare not allow unresolved conflicts to fester or condone moral compromise. But the goal is restoration – inclusion, not exclusion.

---

[13] Murray, *Post-Christendom*, 47, 68, 127–8, 156–7.
[14] See further Murray, *Post-Christendom*, 169–70.
[15] Matthew 18:15–17; cf. Matthew 5:23–34.
[16] See, for example, 1 Corinthians 5:5–8; 11:28–31; 2 Thessalonians 3:14; 1 Timothy 5:20; Revelation 2:14–25.

What issues require confrontation? Another Christendom legacy is the pernicious idea that some sins are inherently worse than others. Roman Catholic categories were 'mortal' or 'venial' sins. Calvin differentiated 'intolerable offences' from 'tolerable faults'. Some churches emphasise personal morality; others are more concerned about social justice. Some sins attract particular opprobrium in certain social contexts. Behaviour regarded as sinful in one culture may be acceptable in another. Remembering which Baptists do not smoke but drink alcohol, which smoke but do not drink, which both drink and smoke and which do neither taxes the memory of those who travel around the global Baptist community! Emerging churches sense that some evangelical churches are obsessed with personal (especially sexual) morality but unconcerned about global, ecological, economic and socio-political issues. Postmodern culture raises various ethical questions, inviting us to re-examine our convictions and distinguish biblical principles from cultural assumptions.

The New Testament gives no exhaustive list of issues requiring church discipline.[17] Jesus simply says 'if your brother or sister sins against you …' The process he outlines is clear but lacks detail. Loving confrontation is relational, not legalistic. The focus is on the integrity of the community and the well-being of our brothers and sisters. The *impact* of certain behaviour on individuals or the church and how they *respond* when confronted may be more significant than the precipitating issue. This process requires contextual awareness, cultural discernment, biblical reflection, relational sensitivity and pastoral nous. Seemingly trivial issues can set in motion a train of events causing serious damage.

---

[17] Specific examples are sexual immorality, idleness, blaspheming, false teaching, divisiveness, idolatry, discontent, slander, drunkenness and financial dishonesty.

Churches that practise loving confrontation well *learn* to do this. They explore ethical and cultural questions, think through the implications of the process and covenant to practise this. Waiting until a crisis appears is unhelpful. Trying to impose this process on a church that has not agreed to it is disastrous. Some Anabaptist churches, therefore, linked church discipline with baptism: those who were baptised committed themselves to give and receive 'fraternal admonition'.[18] Emerging churches can establish it from the outset and teach it in induction courses. Inherited churches will need to broach the subject and agree to explore it together.

Speaking the truth in love

Whether we call it church discipline or loving confrontation, how does this process actually work? Matthew 18:15–17 provides our biblical foundation, although other texts add further perspectives and show the process in operation.[19]

> If your brother or sister sins against you, go and show them their fault, just between the two of you. If they listen to you, you have won them over. But if they will not listen, take one or two others along, so that 'every matter may be established by the testimony of two or three witnesses.' If they refuse to listen

---

[18] See Balthasar Hubmaier, 'A Christian Instruction' in Walter Klaassen, *Anabaptism in Outline: Selected Primary Sources (Classics of the Radical Reformation)* (Scottdale: Herald Press, 1981), 214.

[19] For example: Matthew 5:23; Romans 15:14; 1 Corinthians 5:1–13; Galatians 2:11–14; Philippians 4:2-3; Colossians 3:16; 1 Thessalonians 5:14; 2 Thessalonians 3:6, 14–15; 1 Timothy 5:19–20; Titus 3:10; James 5:19.

to them, tell it to the church; and if they refuse to listen even to the church, treat them as you would a pagan or a tax collector.

Detailed biblical exegesis and exploration of the many pastoral and practical issues this process raises would require another book.[20] But Jesus outlines four steps:

- Go to your brother or sister.
- Take one or two others along.
- Tell it to the church.
- Treat them as pagans or tax collectors.

He gives no guidelines about how to take each step or how long to allow before proceeding to the next. But there are markers:

- The process begins in private and becomes public only if matters cannot be resolved in private.
- Once the brother or sister starts to 'listen' (this word appears four times), there is no need to proceed to the next step.
- The aim throughout is to 'win over' the brother or sister, to achieve restoration and reconciliation.
- There is no mention of church leaders. This is not a process leaders impose or members delegate to them but an expression of reciprocal pastoral care.

---

[20] The few recent books on this unpopular subject are mostly out of print. See especially John White and Ken Blue, *Healing the Wounded: The Costly Love of Church Discipline* (Leicester: Inter-Varsity Press, 1985); Donald Bridge, *Spare the Rod and Spoil the Church* (Bromley: MARC, 1985); Marlin Jeschke, *Disciplining in the Church: Recovering a Ministry of the Gospel* (Scottdale: Herald Press, 1988) and Stuart Murray, *Explaining Church Discipline* (Tonbridge: Sovereign World, 1995). See also www.anabaptistnetwork.com.

- There is no guarantee a brother or sister will listen or be won over. Exclusion from the community is a possibility.

But how do we know when to take step 1? Who should we take along at step 2? What does 'church' mean in step 3? How does exclusion work at step 4? What does it mean to treat people as pagans or tax collectors? So many unanswered questions mean this passage can only provide a framework. Churches that adopt this process must work out together how to interpret and implement it in their own context. Discovering this may be as valuable as practising the process itself.

Other New Testament texts address another crucial issue – the attitude with which we approach every stage of the process. 'Speaking the truth in love' excludes arrogance, judgmentalism and intolerance (which often characterised Christendom-style church discipline). Loving confrontation is exercised with sorrow, as a painful necessity (1 Cor. 5:2); gently and humbly, aware of human weakness (Gal. 6: 1); not in hostility, but in love, an expression of commitment to each other (2 Thes. 3:15). In the language of Ephesians 4: 'Be completely humble and gentle; be patient, bearing with one another in love. Make every effort to keep the unity of the Spirit through the bond of peace.'

These texts help us interpret Matthew 18. 'Go to your bother or sister' is not prompted by spite, antagonism or refusal to accept differences but by concern for them. 'Taking one or two others' is not to rally support but because we value their discernment and recognise we may have misread the situation. 'Telling it to the church' does not imply 'naming and shaming' but allows the community to rehearse its core values and invite everyone to embrace these afresh. At each step the process hopes for resolution and restoration.

The enigmatic reference to 'pagans and tax collectors' helps us understand the fourth step, why the process is necessary and how it fosters churches that are both honest and open. A realistic process designed for fallible communities recognises that restoration is not always achieved. Churches then face two alternatives: to compromise their core values and allow unresolved issues to poison them; or to act with integrity, refusing to collude in destructive behaviour, and review the status of those who will not 'listen to the church'.

Pagans and tax collectors were first-century outsiders: treating someone as a pagan or tax collector meant no longer regarding them as belonging to the community. But on Jesus' lips this phrase takes on a further meaning (which would surely not have been lost on the former tax collector who wrote Matthew!): these outsiders were potential insiders that Jesus loved, calling them to repent, follow him and join his community.

This phrase suggests churches must hold two responses in creative tension. They dare not pretend those who contravene their core values and resist loving confrontation still belong within the community. But this judgement is always provisional: 'pagans and tax collectors' are not written off. The community longs for their restoration. Matthew 18 includes the parables of the lost sheep and the unmerciful servant before and after the passage on loving confrontation. Followers of Jesus wander off and behave badly. We need our brothers and sisters, not to pretend all is well or to reject us, but to speak the truth in love so we can be restored. However long we resist, there is always a way back – and the parable of the lost son describes the celebration awaiting those who return.[21]

There are many risks involved in this process. It places enormous responsibility on the community. Wrong

---

[21] Luke 15:11–32.

attitudes and unwise application can do serious damage. So why take these risks? Partly because Jesus tells us to, partly because experience suggests the risks of *not* practising this process are even greater! Churches that sweep problems under the carpet, fudge moral issues, tolerate unresolved conflicts and avoid loving confrontation become unhealthy and unattractive. Matthew 18, Ephesians 4 and the rest of the New Testament make clear that honest and accountable relationships are vital for healthy churches.[22]

A process whose time has come?

Does the demise of Christendom mean we can recover this liberating and community-building process? Yearnings for relational accountability in many emerging churches and the growing popularity of spiritual direction and mentoring may indicate this is a process whose time has come. It may be counter-cultural in an individualistic society, but perhaps it is counter-cultural in the way that is necessary to build and sustain healthy and attractive churches after Christendom.

What kinds of churches can practise this process sensitively and creatively?

- Churches with clear, agreed and deeply owned core values.
- Churches that have worked out how loving confrontation will operate.
- Churches that induct newcomers into this shared understanding.

---

[22] They may also be essential for missional churches. John Howard Yoder suggests church discipline, practised properly, is missionally attractive. See his *Body Politics: Five Practices of the Christian Community Before the Watching World* (Scottdale: Herald, 2001).

- Churches that are realistic about the struggles individuals and communities face.
- Churches that foster deep, gracious, forgiving and patient friendships.
- Churches whose community life is so rich that no longer belonging provokes soul-searching and changed attitudes.

There is one further criterion: *churches that are not unhealthily dependent on leaders*. The absence of leaders from Matthew 18:15–17 is crucial. In Christendom, church discipline was imposed by leaders on their congregations: it was an exercise of clerical power, however well-intentioned and pastorally sensitive it may sometimes have been. Such power dynamics need not distort loving confrontation in post-Christendom churches. The process works better and builds stronger communities if leaders neither intervene too early nor encourage others to pass the buck to them rather than confronting sisters or brothers as Jesus instructs. Leaders will inevitably, and rightly, become involved in the third and fourth steps, but even here their responsibility is to ensure the process is handled well, rather than taking over.

Centred-set churches are, contrary to what many assume, more suited to this process than others. They have deeply owned core values that shape the community. They are relationally oriented and less likely to apply the process legalistically. They are better able *both* to preserve the integrity of the community *and* to communicate acceptance of those struggling to follow Jesus. They are less concerned about what stage people have reached on their spiritual journey than about the direction in which they are travelling. Bounded-set churches are too inflexible; open-set churches have no basis on which to confront; and fuzzy-set churches will become confused and confusing if they try to practise this. But centred-set churches can practise loving confrontation in ways that allow messy forms of belonging, believing and behaving within an honest and open community.

Harmonious Churches

Loving confrontation is an aspect of 'harmonious' church life. The image of harmony evokes the Ephesians 4 vision of a multi-gifted, interactive, reciprocal, multi-voiced community. In *Post-Christendom* I identify other aspects of harmonious church and its Christendom distortions:[23]

- Interactive learning, rather than reliance on monologue sermons.
- Multi-voiced worship, rather than front-led performances.
- Reciprocal economics, rather than centralised tithing.
- Empowering leadership, rather than disempowering clericalism.

We could explore each topic as fully as we have loving confrontation, noting parallels and how they reinforce each other.[24] The attention given to loving confrontation does not imply it is more important than other topics. But it is the least obviously attractive practice and the most seriously warped by the Christendom mindset.

---

[23] Murray, *Post-Christendom*, 261–74. This includes a short discussion of church discipline.

[24] *Post-Christendom* examines interactive learning. Another book in this series will investigate multi-voiced worship. Reciprocal economics is explored in Stuart Murray, *Beyond Tithing* (Carlisle: Paternoster, 2000).

Once we recognise the significance of harmonious ecclesiology, we will review many aspects of church. How has Christendom disempowered and disabled our churches? What reorientation is needed to develop multi-voiced communities? What processes will prevent us reverting to mono-voiced ecclesiology?

There have been many attempts to introduce multi-voiced ecclesiology, but most have reverted to mono-voiced practices. The gradual retreat in charismatic churches from multi-voiced worship and freely exercised spiritual gifts to dominant and controlling worship leaders is typical. Christendom toxins are not the only problem: low-quality participation, laziness, sloppiness, misguided notions of 'excellence' and increasingly complex liturgy all encourage reversion to less participative patterns. Contributions in house groups in inherited churches and in small-scale emerging churches can be banal and it is difficult to avoid stagnation. It is tempting to regard multi-voiced ecclesiology as unsatisfactory and unsustainable, and to copy thriving cathedral congregations where participation is neither needed nor wanted.

But there are incentives to develop processes that sustain multi-voiced churches:

- Church leavers express dissatisfaction with monologue sermons, performance-oriented worship and non-consultative leadership.
- Those joining churches via process evangelism courses relish opportunities to ask questions and participate in discussion.
- Serious existing and impending leadership shortages require greater sharing of responsibilities, regardless of ecclesial preferences.
- Emerging churches are developing multi-voiced worship and alternatives to monologues, practising

communal hermeneutics and group preparation for events, affirming artists and poets, photographers and sculptors, and valuing the contributions of those on the margins.

• 'Gift-orientated lay ministry' is, despite struggles to sustain this, the strongest factor in British churches that have completed an NCD assessment.

But the harmonious church Ephesians 4 envisions, in which diverse gifts build up the community, does not emerge or evolve automatically. It needs an equipping process to 'prepare God's people for works of service', which involves apostles, prophets, evangelists, pastors and teachers (vv. 11–12).

Leadership dependency

Are these church leaders? This assumption is widespread in inherited and emerging churches. Ephesians 4:11 figures prominently in recent books on church leadership.[25] But leadership is not mentioned in Ephesians 4 (except Christ as the church's head), any more than in Matthew 18. Is this another Christendom legacy – the tendency to import leaders into texts where they are not mentioned because our ecclesiology is dependent on leaders? Are apostles unable to pioneer without leadership positions? Cannot prophets exercise their gifts from the margins rather than the centre? Must evangelists be leaders? Do pastors or teachers need leadership status? These gifts *may* overlap with leadership but in other New Testament gift lists, leadership is either, as here, not mentioned (1 Cor. 12:28) or included alongside other gifts (Rom. 12:4–8).

---

[25] For example, Robinson and Smith, *Invading* and Frost and Hirsch, *Shaping*.

This is not to suggest church leaders were unnecessary in pre-Christendom or will be redundant in post-Christendom. There are many New Testament references to leaders and attempts by some emerging churches to abolish leadership structures have been discouraging. But we must beware importing Christendom assumptions into New Testament texts and Christendom toxins into post-Christendom. One of these toxins is the belief that the emergence or evolution of post-Christendom churches depends *primarily* on church leaders.

In many churches leaders are under huge pressure to perform. Churches hire youth leaders to reach young people and evangelists to enlarge their congregations. They appoint worship leaders to ensure 'corporate' worship is inspiring. They expect their ministers to be attentive pastors and to develop strategies to reverse long-term decline, but demand well-crafted sermons each week, whose preparation uses up an inordinate amount of their time. As Christendom fades, unhealthy dependence on leaders will produce dysfunctional churches and take a heavy toll on leaders. Many leaders will become scapegoats for their churches' failure to adapt to a changing context, blamed for the decline that is taking place for reasons beyond their control.

In Christendom, church leaders were central, and church historians usually emphasise their importance.[26] This perspective has persisted in the final decades of Christendom and will, if unchallenged, distort expectations of church after Christendom. Mission strategists insist that gifted leaders are the key to church growth and to the success or

---

[26] The philosopher Goethe once complained: 'What do I have to do with church history? I don't see anything but parsons. How it goes with the Christians, the ordinary people, about that I can find nothing.'

failure of church planting initiatives.[27] There is substantial evidence to support this assertion – but it needs interpretation. Has church growth and church planting been unhealthily dependent on leaders? Might more churches grow and more church plants succeed if we broke this dependency culture and empowered multi-gifted churches?

Ephesians 4 focuses not on church leaders (even if the five named gifts *are* leadership roles) but on a harmonious church. This empowered community engages in works of service. Its multidimensional activities result in the church functioning properly and becoming mature. It is a long way from this to clerical models in which laity support gifted clergy, who perform works of service. These models exalt – or exhaust – those designated as leaders and disempower the community.

The recovery of apostles, prophets and evangelists (in Christendom only pastors and teachers were recognised) is critical for the emergence of a missional church. These neglected gifts must be restored if churches are to be healthy and properly balanced. But the Christendom mindset affects the interpretation and application of these gifts. Apostolic leadership, in particular, is prone to hierarchical and patriarchal expression, as specially gifted men are hailed as quasi-messianic figures who will lead churches towards growth, social influence and revival. This characterised some branches of the House Church movement in the 1970s and 1980s and reappeared in the 1990s in the 'New Apostolic Churches'.[28]

---

[27] A recent example is Robinson and Smith, *Invading*, 85.

[28] See, for example, C. Peter Wagner (ed.), *The New Apostolic Churches* (Ventura: Regal, 1998); *Churchquake: The Explosive Power of the New Apostolic Reformation* (Ventura: Regal, 2000) and David Cannistraci, *Apostles and the Emerging Apostolic Movement* (Ventura: Regal, 1996).

'Apostolic leadership' is advocated as a liberating alternative to bureaucratic ecclesial patterns. If missional churches are to emerge, we sorely need lightweight networking arrangements to replace cumbersome hierarchical structures. But the apostolic model cannot deliver this. It signals reversion to an ethos that is anathema to most emerging churches and many church leavers.

> Of all the charges laid at the door of the church by many disaffected young people ... the most frequent and damning is the charge of controlling leadership ... stifling creativity, stunting innovation and imagination, forcing uniformity, silencing dissent.[29]

Furthermore, this model requires brilliant and outstanding leaders – who are in short supply. Already, churches searching for new ministers are rejecting unexceptional but able candidates, awaiting a saviour-figure to lead them towards the promised land, or back to their glory days. Most church leaders, however, are faithful but average. This is true of preachers. Occasionally they preach wonderful sermons, but only the most gifted produce these consistently: the dominance of the sermon means many churches experience mediocre preaching. Interactive learning, with fewer sermons contributing more effectively, relieves pressure on preachers and empowers churches de-skilled by dependence on sermons. This translates into other areas of church life: leadership dependency harms leaders and churches alike.

Leadership after Christendom

Emphasising gifted leaders rather than multi-gifted communities and assuming such leaders are 'on the front

---

29 Kelly, *Retrofuture*, 212.

line'[30] are hallmarks of revamped Christendom ecclesiology. Leith Anderson comments wryly: 'Frankly, we
have had many years of church history in which the leaders
of the church have seen the church as the end and the people
as the means.'[31] The Christendom mindset is pervasive and
tenacious. Christendom toxins will not be purged by changing terminology or structure alone. But in marginal
churches, reading Ephesians 4 as envisioning a harmonious
community makes more sense. The role of leaders in
post-Christendom churches – operating accountably in a
team context with others whose gifts and perspectives are
different – is to empower rather than perform, develop
processes to sustain the community and equip those who
really are on the front line.

In many churches team leadership is supplanting solo
leadership. This is consonant with the ubiquitous New Testament pattern of plural leadership and offers churches
greater resources for equipping and empowerment. But
gifted leadership teams can disempower communities even
more comprehensively! However, team ministry is often
nominal or under-developed; many teams lack healthy
diversity; and reversion to solo leadership is common.[32]

Tools measuring church health now recognise the
value of leadership that empowers rather than performs.
NCD's questionnaire invites respondents to agree or
disagree with the dependency-oriented statement 'our
minister has an inspiring and contagious optimism', but
it includes in its quality characteristics 'empowering

---

[30] For example, C. Peter Wagner, *Prayer Shield: How to inter-
cede for pastors, Christian leaders and others on the front line*
(Tunbridge Wells: Monarch, 1992).
[31] Anderson, *21st Century*, 49.
[32] The *Building Bridges of Hope* programme reports
over-optimism about the reality of team leadership and lay participation.

leadership'. Notably, this characteristic generally registers as the weakest element in British churches using the programme.

In post-Christendom, we must *reconfigure* and *de-emphasise* leadership if churches are to be harmonious and healthy.

Reconfiguring leadership raises questions about the kinds of leaders currently in post, in training or applying to become leaders. Some may discover that their skills are unsuited to the nature of leadership in post-Christendom churches. Those who select and train leaders face the challenge of prioritising the skills needed for future church over those that have served inherited churches well.[33] Networkers, community theologians, team-builders, spiritual directors, mentors, coaches and trainers who equip others may be more valuable than public performers.

Some emerging churches are already reconfiguring leadership. This mostly reflects postmodern aversion to authority, rather than sensitivity to the Christendom legacy, but some changes are conducive to post-Christendom ecclesiology:

- Many neither can nor wish to support full-time paid leaders, so responsibilities are more widely shared.
- Some operate rotating leadership, with people exercising leadership in more functional and less formal ways.
- Many reject professional and hierarchical models in favour of more relaxed, relational and consensual leadership.
- Most value the leadership gifts of women and reject patriarchal models.

---

[33] Cf. the discussion about training in chapter 5.

- Many need leaders whose primary gifts are not preaching or public leadership but networking and equipping others.[34]
- Some replace worship leaders with 'worship curators' or apparently leaderless worship.

De-emphasising leadership will be difficult. Leaders and congregations will collude to ensure the dependency culture remains intact. Insecure leaders already disable many churches: some refuse to lead, sometimes under the pretext of being servant leaders;[35] others domineer. They will find such a prospect very threatening. And churches have already lost through the back door many who found the leadership dependency culture alienating and longed for multi-voiced community. Furthermore, if post-Christendom churches are to become multi-gifted communities, and the mature church Ephesians 4 envisages is to evolve or emerge, training for all (not just leaders) is essential. But we must disavow a Christendom legacy that produces dysfunctional communities.

Healthy, Honest and Harmonious

The Ephesians 4 vision of a healthy, honest and harmonious community is inherently attractive, but is it achievable? Can inherited churches evolve into such communities? Will emerging churches display these characteristics? Can we

---

[34] This discovery has been painful for some leaders, liberating for others.
[35] 'Perhaps the emphasis on "servant leadership" espoused by some pastors has more to do with their insecurity than with their humility': Gibbs and Coffey, *Church Next*, 106.

afford to give this much attention to internal maintenance in a context where we must prioritise mission?

Indeed, the agenda for post-Christendom churches proposed in this and the previous chapter seems demanding. Is it realistic for marginal churches in a post-commitment culture? How can we find time and energy for these various processes and practices?

The short answer is that if marginal churches want to thrive, or even survive, in post-Christendom they will need such processes and practices. Chapter 8 offers a longer answer after we have considered in the next chapter a third dimension of church – worship – which potentially makes further demands.

7

Church After Christendom: Worship

Mission, community – and now worship. The order in which we have investigated these subjects is deliberate, in itself a disavowal of the Christendom shift. During the Christendom era worship was primary, community was secondary and mission was on the periphery. For most people, belonging meant attending worship services, not participating in a counter-cultural community or a missional movement. Mission had little relevance in the heart of a Christianised culture, nor was there any reason to differentiate between the worshipping community on Sundays and the community of family, neighbours and work colleagues throughout the week.

In post-Christendom, mission and community are critical. Without effective mission, church after Christendom will not be marginal but non-existent. Without authentic community, mission will be unsustainable, whether we interpret this in attractional or incarnational terms. The re-integration of believing, behaving and belonging is essential.

What about worship? This aspect of church may have predominated in Christendom, to the detriment of mission and community, but surely we are not suggesting worship should receive less attention in post-Christendom? This would invite howls of protest – insisting that worshipping God must take precedence over building community or engaging in mission – and repeated citations of the only phrase most people know in the Westminster Shorter Catechism ('Man's chief end is to glorify God and enjoy him forever').

But this phrase indicates a broad definition of worship, which is well able to embrace both mission and community. Many people mean by 'worship' a narrower range of activities, often associated with the church community gathering to offer praise and prayer. This is a problem when discussing worship: the term slides between meanings – glorifying God in all dimensions of life, personal spirituality, corporate gatherings, extended singing, sermons and ritual activities. People quickly counter any suggestion that worship in one of these narrower senses receives too much attention by sliding over to a broader definition.

This response misses the point. At issue is the relationship between worship (in one or more of its narrower connotations) and other aspects of Christian discipleship – all of which are to glorify God. During the Christendom era, this relationship was distorted. Maybe in post-Christendom we can work towards a better balance between mission, community and worship. We may also relish the opportunity to re-examine what we do when we worship together as the people of God.[1] We will proceed by interacting with both inherited and emerging churches and by listening to joiners and leavers.

Emerging Church Perspectives

In emerging churches there are cross-currents on the subject of worship that may help us identify significant issues for

---

[1] This chapter will generally use 'worship' in one of its narrower senses. See further Alan and Eleanor Kreider, *Worship and Mission after Christendom* (Carlisle: Paternoster, forthcoming).

church after Christendom.[2] As in previous chapters, listening to emerging churches does not imply that church after Christendom will emerge rather than evolve, nor that the current wave of emerging churches represent the church's future. But these churches are emerging in the ruins of Christendom and, if nothing else, offer alternative ways of configuring mission, community and worship.

Worship-oriented churches

New churches have emerged in the past decade motivated primarily by a search for culturally attuned forms of corporate worship that worshippers find authentic. The 'alternative worship' movement is a high-profile expression of emerging church, one of few actual 'movements' within this disparate phenomenon. Indeed, some observers equate alt.worship with emerging church. This is unhelpful. There are many emerging churches where mission or community are primary. And there are several expressions of emerging church in the 'worship-oriented' category: mono-ethnic and multicultural churches, churches developing contextual liturgy, multi-congregational and menu churches, and new forms of monasticism.

These churches offer varied (and some mutually exclusive) perspectives on worship, but they highlight significant issues for post-Christendom churches.

Post-Christendom worship will embrace both *diversity* and *unity*.[3] Worship-oriented emerging churches take different approaches on this issue. Multi-congregational and menu churches offer diverse expressions of worship, tailored to particular groups of worshippers, but they try to

---

[2] This section should be read in conjunction with chapter 3.
[3] Although not primarily about worship, this dual emphasis is at the heart of the Ephesians 4 vision of a mature church.

hold these together within one church community. This is a refreshing change from the inflexibility and uniformity of the Christendom era. It represents a determined attempt to be culturally sensitive without abandoning efforts to embody the culture-transcending unity to which several New Testament passages point. But mono-ethnic churches and churches developing contextual liturgy prioritise diversity, conscious that multicultural church is presently more hope than reality, and wary of co-option into a united church that marginalises their cultural distinctives. If we are to pursue the ecumenical vision of a united church in a non-imperialistic way that befits our post-Christendom context, we must hear the concerns of these churches and explore more creative, and patient, ways forward. Perhaps it is unhelpful to over-emphasise the significance of worshipping together. We might discover and express our unity in Christ more effectively through shared mission or shared meals.

Post-Christendom worship will be both *centred* and *decentred*. Visitors to alt.worship events may struggle to identify who is 'leading' them or even which way to face. This is not accidental. Among several 'alternative' elements in these communities are their multidirectional, individualised and decentred approach to worship and their aversion to front-led events. They use liturgical resources from the Christendom era, but their ethos represents a critique of worship-as-clerical-performance, whether in inherited churches or charismatic events dominated by worship leaders. Radically decentred worship events, however, will not suffice for post-Christendom Christians. Marginal communities need truly corporate worship to sustain their common life, nurture their discipleship, renew their vision and energise their mission. Perhaps the new monastic communities provide a helpful counter-balance.

Post-Christendom worship will be both *culturally attuned* and *counter-cultural*. Some critics of alt.worship events, contextual liturgy and mono-ethnic churches accuse them of capitulating to their cultural context. This accusation may simply reflect the critics' unwitting and unrecognised capitulation to a different cultural context! What some critics regard as counter-cultural is often simply old-fashioned. In a diverse and changing culture, cultural attunement is the initial stage in missional engagement. Those who are developing forms of worship that engage with postmodern or youth subcultures, for example, must risk cultural capitulation to become culturally attuned. The path to counter-cultural worship runs through culturally attuned worship. However, if it never reaches this destination, the critics have a point. True worship is profoundly counter-cultural, calling worshippers to embrace an alternative vision, deviant values and a different metanarrative with implications for both mission and community. 'Jesus is Lord' is a profoundly political statement that relativises all other sources of authority.

Post-Christendom worship will be both *creative* and *sustainable*. The time and energy devoted to preparing for worship events in some emerging churches is remarkable, as is the creativity that shapes these events. Multi-congregational and menu churches, as well as alt.worship events,[4] require more preparation than formal or informal worship in most inherited churches. They involve many people and value diverse gifts (some rarely used in inherited churches). Empowerment and creativity characterise many emerging churches. But marginal churches must ensure worship is also sustainable.[5] Marginality inspires fresh

---

[4] And seeker-oriented churches, though these are motivated primarily by mission.

[5] See further chapter 8.

ways of worshipping but also implies limited resources. Some emerging churches are already experiencing exhaustion and creativity-fatigue. Constant innovation is unsustainable over the long haul. It also deflects time and creative energy from building community and engaging in mission.

Mission- and community-oriented churches

Emerging churches motivated by community and mission factors may appear to have fewer perspectives on worship. Their creative energy focuses on community-building or missional dimensions of church. But this may be significant. Perhaps, unwittingly, these churches are reacting against the preoccupation with worship that marginalised community and mission in the Christendom era. They raise further issues with which post-Christendom churches will wrestle.

For whom do churches design their corporate worship? Worship-oriented churches may not be indifferent to those who do not belong, but many are concerned primarily about designing worship that is congenial to existing members. Some mono-ethnic churches want people from other ethnic groups to join them, but few will adapt their worship style to accommodate them. Those who plan alt.worship events often insist that authenticity, not accessibility, is critical: they design worship for those who already belong. Some mission-oriented churches suggest worship should emerge, at least in part, from interaction with people beyond the church; if it is rooted in their culture, they may own it. Those involved in network, youth, culture-specific and indigenous neighbourhood churches prioritise the preferences of those who do not yet belong (some even plant churches in which the worship style is uncongenial to the planters but contextually appropriate). If belonging continues to precede believing for many people and interest in spirituality is a doorway to Christian faith, post-Christendom churches, as they design their corporate worship, must balance the needs of present and potential members. Authenticity and accessibility are both important.

How sustainable is multi-voiced worship? Some emerging churches are convinced that multi-voiced worship promotes spiritual growth and builds stronger communities. But many churches that introduce multi-voiced worship find almost irresistible the gravitational pull of the mono-voiced Christendom legacy. Table churches, household churches, cell churches and other small-scale community-oriented churches know the difficulties of sustaining multi-voiced worship.[6] Many struggle with the low quality and predictability of contributions. Multi-voiced churches do not just happen.[7] But there is an alternative to reverting to mono-voiced worship – training and equipping processes that 'prepare God's people for works of service'. These 'works of service' and the various 'gifts of grace' (Eph. 4:7) are for mission and community building as well as worship, but they do sustain multi-voiced worship. Some emerging churches agree with Ephesians 4 that maturity comes not through over-dependence on worship leaders or listening to endless monologues, but 'as each part does its work' (v. 16), contributing distinctively to the harmony.

How can churches integrate worship and daily life? Many church leavers disembark because what happens on Sundays is unrelated to the rest of their lives. In 321 the emperor Constantine made Sunday a day of rest. This released Christians from the demands of work; they no longer needed to worship together early in the morning or after

---

[6] Most cell churches combine participatory small-group worship and less participatory celebrations.

[7] Cf. chapter 6.

the day's work was done. But it also disconnected worship and work. Workplace churches are an attempt to reconnect these elements. We considered other strategies in chapter 5. Midweek church also abandons Sundays, incorporating worship into existing community groups or shared activities. New monasticism represents another way of configuring worship by integrating personal and corporate spiritual rhythms into daily life. Other ways of addressing this will emerge as post-Christendom churches respond to the challenge of developing patterns of worship that are not detached or escapist but 'prepare God's people for works of service' in their daily lives.

Is involvement in corporate worship essential? 'Belonging' in Christendom meant, above all, attending worship services. The community and mission dimensions were optional for most people. In some emerging churches, where mission or community are primary, corporate worship has become an optional extra. Christians involved in community projects or working for social justice may regard this as an alternative to involvement in corporate worship. Seven-days-a-week churches may not differentiate between those who worship together and those who participate in other aspects of church life. For some Christians involved in dispersed church or 'parachurch' groups, participation in the corporate worship of a local congregation is secondary or optional. These may be understandable reactions to overemphasis on worship at the expense of mission and community in many inherited (and some emerging) churches. But are they overreactions? Are they sustainable in post-Christendom? Or will Christians and churches that downgrade corporate worship struggle to survive on the margins of an alien environment?

Church beyond the congregation

Many Christians are confident that they can survive, even thrive, without participating in corporate worship. This is the stance of church leavers, who meet informally with like-minded friends, and of some post-church groups. Some report new opportunities, time and enthusiasm to engage in mission or various community initiatives beyond the congregation, now that they have disengaged from the demands of church. Once they have got beyond the disorientation that most leavers experience who no longer participate in corporate worship, many revel in their new-found freedom and wonder why they remained committed for so long to something so unedifying and frustrating. Since many such leavers are well-established and deeply rooted Christians, their years of corporate worship have undoubtedly imparted sufficient resources to sustain them for some time.[8]

But, just as it is too soon to assess the long-term sustainability of emerging churches, it is also too soon to judge whether those who have left churches during the past few years can thrive, or even survive long term, without corporate worship. Is the relaxed and congenial experience of eating, talking (and maybe praying) with friends enough to sustain discipleship in post-Christendom? Is corporate worship alongside those who are different actually essential for spiritual growth?[9] What about the leavers' children or oth-

---

[8] But this ignores the impact of their withdrawal from corporate worship on others who have not left the church.

[9] 'The wonder of the church is that it is full of people I wouldn't normally meet, wouldn't have the opportunity to choose as friends, and would never hear speaking about their relationship with Jesus': Simon Jones, *Why Bother with Church?: The Struggle to Belong* (Leicester: Inter-Varsity Press, 2001), 125. This is an issue also for many small-scale and homogeneous churches.

ers who (perhaps through the leavers' witness) embark on Christian discipleship without corporate worship to sustain them? Will some post-church groups inevitably reinvent corporate worship and evolve into new churches?

Church beyond the Congregation by Australian Jim Thwaites has been influential in both the New Churches and some emerging churches.[10] This book is far from clear in its arguments and conclusions, but Thwaites urges Christians to reject all aspects of Platonic dualism and recover the Hebraic worldview that Hellenism supplanted. A classic example of dualism, he argues, is overemphasis on church-as-congregation, distracting Christians from the spheres of family, work and the world beyond the congregation.

Thwaites' interpretation of Ephesians 4 has much in common with its interpretation in Part Two of this book. He writes: 'the equipping of saints for works of service was for all of life, rather than primarily an equipping for local church life' and 'leaders are called to be servants of the saints, equipping them for every good work in creation. As such the saints' works are more important than that of the leaders.'[11] He also endorses concerns raised in previous chapters about the inadequacy of the label 'parachurch', over-dependence on monologue sermons and churches spending money mainly on internal programmes.[12] Furthermore, he traces the problem of dualism to the fourth century, implying it resulted from the Christendom shift.[13] It is tempting to endorse his approach wholeheartedly as the way forward for church after Christendom.

---

[10] Thwaites, *Beyond the Congregation*, first mentioned in chapter 1. See also *Renegotiating*.
[11] Thwaites, *Renegotiating*, 73, 81–2.
[12] Thwaites, *Renegotiating*, 20–1, 87, 190.
[13] Thwaites, *Renegotiating*, 10.

But there are problems with his argument – or at least with the way many interpret it. The influence of Platonic dualism on the church as it encountered Hellenistic culture certainly caused problems (although mission in Hellenistic culture required cultural attunement as well as counter-cultural critique and Hellenism need not be denigrated in the way some propose).[14] But the influence of dualism on the church predated the fourth-century Christendom shift. Christendom, in fact, was a sacral culture which *rejected* dualism in favour of a holistic creation-wide worldview, similar to that which Thwaites advocates. Thwaites argues for a Hebraic approach but (like Christendom) rejects an essential element of the Hebraic worldview – which envisions the renewal of creation by means of the work and witness of a distinctive and hopeful community, sustained by counter-cultural worship.

The biblical story involves a distinctive community within creation (Israel among the nations; churches scattered throughout the world), modelling an alternative vision and living by different values. If members of this community are to remain distinctive in an alien environment, they need to be *gathered* as well as *dispersed*. Community-building practices and processes are essential. So too is corporate worship, in which the community rehearses the biblical story, rekindles its vision of a renewed creation and prays for the coming of God's kingdom.

Abandoning corporate worship or relegating this to insignificance (as some conclude from Thwaites' writings) may hold out the promise of releasing Christians to work for social transformation. But this sounds suspiciously like Christendom reinvented.[15] A society-wide (or creation-

---

[14] Not least because Hellenistic influences are already apparent in the Greek New Testament.

[15] It is also individualistic, which is hardly Hebraic!

wide) strategy is exactly what fourth-century church leaders exchanged for the pre-Christendom strategy of planting throughout society distinctive communities that modelled (albeit imperfectly) God's intentions for all. Christendom had what theologians call an 'over-realised eschatology', supplanting Jesus' risky and unimpressive 'mustard-seed' approach with a strategy to revolutionise the whole of society. Within this strategy church-as-congregation had no distinctive or inspirational role. This ambitious programme was a catastrophic failure. It corrupted both church and society.

Christendom's capacity to reappear in various guises is remarkable! Abandoning or marginalising church-as-congregation, and especially corporate worship, in favour of 'church beyond the congregation' may attract Christians who are tired of the demands of many congregations and the escapism of some corporate worship. But Christians on the margins in post-Christendom will be unable to sustain kingdom-oriented social transformation (or even discern what this might look like) without the flawed but vital witness of distinctive Christian communities. Indeed, post-Christendom churches will not survive except as distinctive communities, sustained by counter-cultural corporate worship.

The argument in this chapter, then, is not that we should abandon corporate worship but that we should de-emphasise it and discover a healthier balance between mission, community and worship.[16] De-emphasising worship might also reduce the frequency and passion of congregational conflict over styles of worship.[17] In

---

[16] Just as chapter 6 advocated that we should de-emphasise, not abolish, church leadership.

[17] This is the argument in Pearse and Matthews, *We must stop meeting like this ....*

post-Christendom marginal churches cannot afford to be absorbed with such internal dissension. As Leith Anderson warns, 'the twenty-first century church must be less preoccupied with internal issues, petty conflicts and traditional divisions ... luxuries of affluence and of a religious culture.'[18]

But de-emphasising worship means neither undervaluing it nor being careless about its focus, content and direction. As many emerging churches have found, this is where inherited churches come into their own. Within their diverse traditions are glorious resources and wise perspectives, refined over many centuries. The Christendom shift may have introduced toxins into the liturgical practices of the churches and distorted the balance between worship, community and mission; but the Christendom era has bequeathed an enduring legacy of powerful rituals, stirring music, remarkable art and poetry and beautifully crafted liturgy, rooted in deep spirituality.

Inherited Church Resources

As a church planting consultant I frequently encounter young churches that dismantle inherited patterns of worship, then (usually about two years later) re-appropriate many abandoned practices. Exhausted by innovating and not fully satisfied with the results, they re-examine inherited forms of worship and begin to appreciate why these have stood the test of time. Just as cultural attunement should precede cultural critique and counter-cultural responses, so experimentation and even some iconoclasm may need to precede re-appropriation of enduring worship practices. But a sustainable pattern is often a blend of old and new, sensitively contextualised.

---

[18] Anderson, *21st Century*, 20.

Reactions and re-appropriation

Some emerging churches react less strongly to historic practices than recent forms of worship, especially those found in charismatic churches. Their critique overlaps with the complaints of many church leavers:

- Front-led and stage-managed performances that may disempower, manipulate and infantilise congregations (contrary to the early charismatic impetus).
- Interpreting 'worship' as extended periods of singing, with content that often is banal and repetitive, sometimes romanticised or even semi-erotic.[19]
- An incessantly upbeat mood with little sensitivity to events beyond the church and no room for other moods – especially contemplation, reflection, lament, anger or uncertainty.[20]
- Overemphasis on immanence at the expense of transcendence and mystery.
- Lengthy monologue sermons, often poorly researched and simplistic in their theology, psychology and social commentary.
- Over-emphasis on the verbal at the expense of the visual and on informality rather than symbolism and ritual.

---

[19] Memorably characterised by Sam Hargreaves in his London School of Theology dissertation as 'Jesus is my girlfriend' worship. A nameless Oxford theologian describes it as homo-erotic worship!

[20] See further John Bell, 'The Lost Tradition of Lament' in Stephen Darlington and Alan Kreider (eds.), *Composing Music for Worship* (Norwich: Canterbury Press, 2003).

- Imprisonment within a subculture that is poorly attuned to a plural postmodern society.

Deeply disenchanted by this worship genre, some emerging churches experiment with alternative approaches and delve deeply into church history for ancient resources and practices, remixing and contextualising them in sometimes startling ways.[21] This has not only enriched these churches but has acted as a stimulus to charismatic churches, many of which now integrate such practices into their own worship, and has rekindled the enthusiasm of some inherited churches for their own traditions.

This re-appropriation of inherited church practices and resources is welcome, but it provokes two questions. First, the allergic reaction to charismatic worship evident in some emerging churches is rather indiscriminate. Are there not valuable aspects of charismatic worship that they might also re-appropriate? Multi-voiced communities, exercising spiritual gifts, offering exuberant praise, emotionally engaged in worship, unconstrained by fixed patterns and consciously open to the Spirit – these elements may be of lasting value if we can detach them from aspects of charismatic culture that many find trite and nauseating. Second, is eclectic but rather uncritical appropriation of resources and practices from the Christendom era dangerous? Have Christendom toxins been purged, or will they sooner or later infect emerging churches? We must ask the same question as we propose here elements of inherited church worship that can sustain church after Christendom

---

[21] Alt.worship events, for instance, draw on sources as diverse as 'Celtic' spirituality, the music of Taizé, the contemplative tradition, creation spirituality, Anglo-Catholicism and feminist and liberationist hermeneutics.

Rhythms and resources

The scope of liturgical resources from past centuries means that this section can only be indicative and selective. In light of the proposal that post-Christendom churches re-balance worship, community and mission, we will concentrate on those practices that enhance the missional and communal dimensions of the worshipping congregation:

- *Corporate Bible reading.* Hearing substantial portions of the biblical text read aloud regularly, with or without exposition, earths the community in the story of God's mission, within which it finds its own identity and destiny. Reading widely and extensively, rather than selectively and intensively, provides some protection against narrow vision and distorted emphases. This rhythm will be increasingly important in post-Christendom for Christians not as steeped in the biblical story as previous generations were.
- *Praying the Psalms.* However we do this – in song, responsive reading, chant, with accompanying visual images, rewriting them for our own context – we must resist the temptation to emasculate the psalms by using them selectively. Their narrative content is important and we should not skip these portions; the wide range of moods is essential for authentic worship and we should not edit out anger, doubt, pain and confusion.
- *Corporate songs.* Although 'I' language appears in many psalms, its overuse in contemporary Christian songwriting plagues corporate worship. We may be physically together but our worship is individualistic. This is problematic in charismatic and decentred alt.worship settings. Marginal churches need a

strong corporate identity, fostered by the 'we' language of songs from many traditions.

- *Passing the peace*. The practice may vary in different churches (hugs, kissing the cheek, handshakes, etc.), but this simple liturgical practice, taken seriously, is a community-building practice that makes it harder to hold grudges against other Christians.

- *Corporate intercession*. Praying together – guided by one person, in unison or in small groups – for the world, the global church and the mission purposes of God strengthens the church's missional identity and awareness of belonging to a global community. Through corporate intercession, marginal churches resist contemporary metanarratives, global injustice, redemptive violence and other prevailing ideologies. Praying the subversive Lord's Prayer,[22] they keep alive the hope of a new earth, remain alert to the alluring power of evil and commit themselves to sustaining a healthy, honest and harmonious community.

- *Transcultural liturgy*. As a counter-balance to contextual liturgy, using songs and prayers, stories and rituals from other times and places enhances the sense of belonging to a community across space and time. For marginal churches in post-Christendom, this connectedness and larger perspective is important.

- *Breaking bread and sharing wine*. Known by various names and celebrated very simply or with awesome ritual, this central act of worship combines the elements of mission and community as the reconciled church 'proclaims the Lord's death until he comes'

---

[22] Which, though presented as a resource for private prayer in Matthew 6, uses 'we' language.

(1 Cor. 11:26) and confesses afresh that it is 'one body' (Eph. 4:4). Post-Christendom churches may query why emerging and some inherited churches break bread together infrequently, grieve the enforced separation of Catholics and other Christians who may not break bread together and query restrictions many churches place on those who may participate.[23]

Some emerging churches have incorporated into their worship other inherited church resources, just as some inherited churches have adopted emerging church practices – encouraging examples of symbiosis between inherited and emerging churches. But how can we detect and purge any Christendom toxins?

Reworking and subverting

We may find some clues in the following examples from the Anabaptist tradition that disavowed Christendom. Anabaptists adapted – and sometimes subverted – inherited church resources and recovered neglected practices.

In 1528, shortly before being burned at the stake, Balthasar Hubmaier wrote 'A Form for the Supper of

---

[23] In Christendom, baptism was administered by priests but was indiscriminate, required of everyone. The communion table, in contrast, was protected by rails. Only the priest could preside and, for many centuries, drink the wine. Perhaps in post-Christendom we can review these practices. Those who are moving towards the centre of centred-set churches, wherever they currently are in terms of believing, behaving and belonging, are welcome at the open table hosted by the risen Christ. This table may become the place of commitment, from which new disciples rise to be baptised to express their faith and to commit themselves to follow Jesus.

Christ', an Anabaptist communion liturgy.[24] Most Anabaptists broke bread together simply without set words, so this is an unusual document. Hubmaier used the traditional Catholic Mass as his template but subtly adapted and subverted it. He placed ordinary utensils on the table; he gave instructions for when to sit or kneel that challenged assumptions about the context of worship; he used inclusive language that did not separate or elevate the person leading the congregation; he invited people to ask questions or make further comments after the sermon; and he introduced a new element – the 'pledge of love' by which members committed themselves to love God, one another, their neighbours and their enemies.

Many Anabaptists were hymn writers. Some of the most poignant hymns originated in prisons across Europe, as Anabaptists awaiting trial or execution expressed their faith in songs that their communities learned and sang. Many are rich in narrative, celebrating God's activity in biblical times and in more recent years, especially on the margins and in the suffering of his people. Post-Christendom churches will need such resources if they are to 'sing the Lord's song in a strange land'.[25] Singing church history reminds us that the story of God's mission did not end in the New Testament. Songs written out of suffering and marginalisation may help offset the triumphalism and tyrannical joyfulness that alienates church leavers.

Hubmaier's invitation to his congregation to ask questions and debate with him after his sermon is typical of many Anabaptist congregations, which practised communal biblical interpretation. This practice, which other

---

[24]   This example draws gratefully on Eleanor Kreider, 'The Lord's Supper', *Anabaptism Today* 2 (February 1993), 8–12; also available at www.anabaptistnetwork.com.

[25]   Psalm 137:4.

dissident groups shared, challenged the dominance of the monologue sermon that was a consequence of the Christendom shift. It 'prepared God's people' to wrestle with biblical teaching, argue effectively with inquisitors and apply biblical teaching creatively, rather than mechanistically, to their daily lives.[26] Jim Thwaites, criticising the dominance of sermons, writes: 'Many Christians ... don't need to do much "Christian" thinking because Sunday by Sunday the preacher ... does most of it for them ... It's no wonder that many outside of the faith consider Christians to be opinionated and naïve.'[27] Communal biblical interpretation is another process that does not work properly unless churches learn and practise it; but post-Christendom churches may decide it is worth investing in.

Beyond reworking and subverting traditional practices, Anabaptists also recovered marginalised practices. A well-known example is foot-washing, which Christendom had formalised and clericalised, but which for Anabaptists was a community-building discipline. They also exchanged greetings as people travelled from church to church, carrying news of God's people and God's mission in various places. There are many examples in the New Testament of Christians and churches exchanging greetings[28] – much of the New Testament comprises letters greeting churches or individuals. This practice faded in Christendom, but churches in an alien culture value the exchange of greetings and news of progress or setbacks for their marginal mission

---

[26] See Stuart Murray, *Biblical Interpretation in the Anabaptist Tradition* (Waterloo: Pandora, 2000). For examples of communal biblical interpretation among English radicals, see Christopher Hill, *The World Turned Upside Down* (London: Penguin, 1972), 95, 104–5.

[27] Thwaites, *Renegotiating*, 92–3.

[28] See, for example, Romans 1:7; 16:1–23; 1 Corinthians 1:2–3; 16:19–21.

movement. The hunger in some emerging churches for news of other pioneering initiatives and the enthusiasm with which small churches in different nations receive and send greetings indicates this simple practice may be significant in post-Christendom, encouraging marginal churches and fostering messy relational ecumenism.

Anabaptism did not escape the institutionalisation that creeps up on all movements. It actually succumbed fairly soon, harried and weakened by persecution. Its subversive practices did not entirely disappear (some persisted and echoes of others can still be heard in Anabaptist churches); but as the movement lost missional momentum, there were fewer innovations in worship and some community-building processes turned sour. Church discipline, especially, became perfectionist and more inclined to exclude than restore. Anabaptism offers warning, as well as resources, to post-Christendom churches.

Emerging churches have not mined Anabaptism for liturgical resources in the way they have, for example, the Celtic tradition.[29] Christians in inherited and emerging churches have embraced Anabaptist perspectives on community and mission, but few have explored its perspectives on worship or spirituality. Perhaps the examples in this section will encourage further exploration. The tradition's distinctive emphasis on the life and teaching of Jesus, which many have found inspirational and challenging, infuses Anabaptist spirituality and worship as well as its approach to discipleship. Its multi-voiced worship encourages post-

---

[29] This may, partly, be because less material has been available. Several publications have begun to plug this gap, including Daniel Liechty, *Early Anabaptist Spirituality: Selected Writings* (New York: Paulist Press, 1994) and C. Arnold Snyder, *Following in the Footsteps of Christ: The Anabaptist Tradition (Traditions of Christian Spirituality)* (London: Darton, Longman & Todd, 2004).

Christendom churches to be truly *charismatic*, as each member contributes whatever will build up the body (Eph. 4:7, 16) and truly *liturgical*, for *leitourgeo* implies that worship is the work of God's people.

A final characteristic of Anabaptist worship that is particularly significant for church after Christendom and forms a bridge to the final chapter is simplicity. By contrast with Christendom's complex rituals and the exhausting innovation of some emerging churches, Anabaptist worship was very simple. The perspectives and resources of inherited and emerging churches, the dissident tradition and the global Christian community can enormously enrich worship in post-Christendom churches. But this cornucopia of resources risks re-emphasising, not de-emphasising worship. To be sustainable, post-Christendom worship must also be simple.

8

Church After Christendom
Simple and Sustainable

Sustainability

Chapters 5–7 present a demanding agenda for church after Christendom. But, as noted earlier, this does not pretend to be a comprehensive vision of the church that might emerge or evolve. Those chapters focus on issues the post-Christendom lens reveals with unusual clarity. Different lenses will highlight other, maybe equally important, concerns. There are glaring omissions here, not least the absence of any reference to children in church after Christendom.[1] And further books in the *After Christendom* series will probe more deeply issues introduced here and investigate other topics.

Nevertheless, there is enough here to provoke concerns about sustainability. Some of the proposals involve significant time commitment: process evangelism that starts further back; induction into counter-cultural discipleship and responsible participation in multi-voiced communities;

---

[1] For a recent and wonderfully comprehensive collection of material, see Glenn Miles and Josephine-Joy Wright, *Celebrating Children: Equipping People Working with Children and Young People Living in Difficult Circumstances Around the World* (Carlisle: Paternoster, 2003).

commissioning members who start new jobs; learning to practise loving confrontation; and so on. How can marginal churches with limited resources in a post-commitment culture possibly sustain this kind of church life?

As we address this legitimate question, however, we should ask another: what kind of church can sustain Christians in post-Christendom? We need churches that are not only sustainable but also sustaining.

Clearing the ground

Some ground clearing might help:

- Church after Christendom will not be uniform. The diversity-in-unity model of Ephesians 4 applies not only to individual churches but to the global people of God. Different churches will embody in different ways the strategies, practices and processes suggested in previous chapters, as they reflect on their particular context and participation in God's mission.
- The shape of church after Christendom is less significant than its ethos.[2] Many thousands of Christians have left church in recent years, few of them because they were distressed by its shape or

---

[2] I am not suggesting that there is no connection between shape and ethos. 'Church organization – how the church develops its structures, processes and leadership – is itself a form of witness to the world. It witnesses to the fact that here exists a social community that possesses a spiritual character. It is a witness that a redemptive use of power is possible within a human community. This witness can be either positive or negative': Craig van Gelder, *The Essence of the Church: A Community Created by the Spirit* (Grand Rapids: Baker, 2000), 161.

structure. The main challenge of emerging churches is not their reshaping of church but the different ethos some of them embody. What matters is not specific practices or processes but churches that are healthy, worshipping missional communities.

- The proposals in chapters 5–7 are not meant as additional demands for already overstretched churches. We have resisted the notion of 'bolting on' activities. Church after Christendom needs a sharper focus and a realistic agenda. This will mean doing fewer things or doing them differently, not doing extra things.

- These proposals are tentative and provisional. They indicate the reconfiguring that may be necessary as we move into exile in post-Christendom. Further experience beyond the present transitional zone at the end of Christendom may suggest that some proposals are more valuable than others – and that some are misguided. This may be the calling of some emerging churches: to pioneer on behalf of the church and share what they learn.

Asking questions

Many churches, especially but not only inherited churches, need to review what they are presently doing, and why. The purpose-driven church model encourages this. We can identify activities that do not repay the energy we invest in them, processes that drain rather than sustain us, practices that do not build healthy missional communities. Some activities are almost sacrosanct, protected by deeply vested interests, but we should still apply the 'double sustainability' test: can marginal churches sustain them, and do they sustain marginal churches?

So we might ask (depending on our style of church):

- Need we pack every service with so many different ingredients? If we ensure that each month, or quarter, we have a balanced diet (of teaching, testimony, praise, intercession, prayer for healing, singing, breaking bread, discussion, silence, commissioning, storytelling, news sharing and whatever else we need to sustain community and energise mission), might this not mean more relaxed weekly services and space for new initiatives?
- How many monologue sermons do we need? How many can we digest and act upon? What if we have one well-prepared sermon each month and spend four weeks reflecting together on its implications? Might we then treat sermons far more seriously than we currently do and make more creative use of our time?
- Do we need to sing so many songs? Do extended periods of singing enhance worship, build up the community and equip us for mission and discipleship? What might we do instead if we sang less? Would this be more life-giving?
- Do we need extra meetings for 'church business', which few people attend? Can we integrate the agenda into our praying and worshipping? Or combine it with training on how to exercise discernment as a community? Does it matter if 'non-members' participate or watch, or are we ashamed of how we conduct business?
- How many people need to be involved in institutional maintenance? A common complaint is that 20 per cent of the people do 80 per cent of the work. What if we simplify church life so that 20 per cent is quite sufficient, releasing the 80 per cent for 'works of service' beyond the community?[3]

---

[3] Eddie Gibbs cites this proposal of Robert Slocum. See Gibbs and Coffey, *Church Next*, 89.

- What activities can we suspend while we run training courses and induction processes, rather than squeeze them into an already full schedule? Might short, focused courses be more effective than long-running programmes?
- Do denominations sustain churches or place unsustainable demands on them? Here, too, sustainability is double-edged if we value translocal church relationships and resources. But can we streamline them, dismantle activities that are unsustainable for marginal mission movements and transform them into networks?

Fundamentally, inherited churches need to ask two questions. How much time are we wasting on activities that do not sustain a missional community and will soon become unsustainable? And how much time do we devote to internal activities at the expense of mission beyond the church?

For several years Robert Warren has advocated 'simplifying church life to give people more time to be active outside the church'.[4] Releasing people from absorption with internal activities is essential if churches continue using process evangelism courses, which depend on relationships beyond the church community. But the issue is much broader, unless we limit Christian discipleship to attending meetings. Richard Thomas trenchantly comments, 'Jesus didn't die a painful death on a cross merely to turn us into good churchgoers.'[5] As we move from Christendom to post-Christendom, many churches (and denominations) need to undertake some judicious pruning.[6]

---

[4] Warren, *Signs of Life*, 76. Cf. his other writings.
[5] Thomas, *Counting*, 93.
[6] See John 15:1–2.

What about emerging churches? Some models (seeker-oriented and alt.worship) may be unsustainable – or at least non-reproducible without similar resources and gifted people. Others represent simpler and more sustainable forms of church: clusters that do not try to do everything, cell churches that prioritise people rather than buildings or events, table and household churches that need minimal infrastructure. New monastic communities, however, are more demanding than most inherited churches, and many new churches depend on highly motivated and deeply committed pioneers.

What are church leavers saying? Many report burnout and complain that churches are insensitive to family and work pressures and have unrealistic expectations. Leavers' perspectives are particularly significant since many were for years, or even decades, deeply committed to their churches. Some were even responsible for creating the unsustainable churches they have left! Leavers suggest that many churches are far too busy trying to sustain an institution that will soon be unsustainable and already is not sustaining them. Many argue that inordinate amounts of time spent keeping the show on the road could be better spent building relationships with neighbours, serving their local community or working for peace and justice in a broken world. Adding another twist to familiar categories, excessive 'belonging' may hinder creative and faithful 'behaving'!

Refocusing commitment

We encountered previously a popular description of Western society: many designate it a *post-commitment* culture. Churches are not alone in struggling with questions of sustainability. Political parties, trade unions, voluntary organisations and community groups are all affected. Institutional loyalty, attending numerous meetings and long-term commitment to people and structures – the bread-and-butter of inherited church life – are less congenial than in the past.

But this designation may not be entirely apt. It may be unwise to promote low-commitment churches that demand little but cater for 'church consumers'– and not just because the notion of 'church consumers' is incongruent with the Ephesians 4 vision of participating members who shape their community. Our culture may not be post-commitment; instead it may be inclined to express commitment differently. Passionate advocacy of causes, involvement in social movements, even the popularity of extreme sports may indicate this. High-commitment churches may be counter-cultural in some senses, but they may be attractive *if the commitment involved is rightly focused*.

What might this mean?

- Churches with clear core values – not imposed by leaders but which the whole community shapes and owns.
- Churches with a realistic vision, holistic agenda and sustainable rhythm of worship, mission and community.
- Churches that do not monopolise their members' time and energy but equip them to fulfil their calling, take risks and pursue their dreams beyond the congregation.
- Churches in which all activities and structures are subject to challenge, change and closure if they are no longer sustaining or sustainable.
- Churches that are not besotted by their own survival but operate as missional communities, disbanding or reconfiguring themselves as their context requires.

- Churches shaped and captivated by the biblical story, eschewing quick-fix strategies and not 'tossed back and forth' or 'blown here and there' (Eph. 4:14) by various fads.
- Churches that 'settle down' in exile, 'seek the peace and prosperity' of post-Christendom society and 'do not listen' to unrealistic expectations (Jer. 29:4–10), but wait and pray patiently for the unfolding of God's future.

The deep commitment of those who pioneer new churches or join 'parachurch' groups in order to be wholehearted disciples and missional Christians, rather than remaining in inherited churches, suggests that the real issue is not low commitment but wrongly focused commitment. Many church leavers, too, become deeply committed to other causes, investing in campaigns for social justice, neighbourhood renewal or cultural activities the passion, time and energy they previously devoted to their churches. Post-Christendom churches will struggle to inspire commitment of the kind that previous generations expressed in the form of institutional loyalty. But as communities of faith that sustain multifaceted mission initiatives, vocational ministry and creative cultural engagement, they have a viable future.

Revisiting the categories of 'believing' and 'belonging', post-Christendom Christians will need to 'belong' to churches that sustain our faith in an alternative story if we are to exercise discernment and not 'believe' prevailing cultural myths. As participants in a missional movement we will 'belong' in our society (rather than disengaging), but to maintain our identity as exiles, who ultimately 'belong' to a different kingdom,[7] we will need to 'belong' to

---

[7] Philippians 3:20.

churches that sustain hope in that kingdom and embody its values.

Without a community that (however imperfectly) models counter-cultural values and alternatives practices, social reformers lack integrity. Without a healthy community to which people can belong before believing, evangelists lack credibility. Without an attractive community that recruits, nurtures and envisions people, community activists lack volunteers. Without a worshipping community that sustains faith and hope, many people will lose heart.

But sustainability is two-way. A certain level of maintenance is needed to sustain a community that can, in turn, sustain mission. If its members value the community and recognise its sustaining role, they will invest in its maintenance. But they will not if such maintenance becomes excessive or self-absorbed. That kind of church will be unsustainable in post-Christendom.

Simplicity

Many church leavers are simply exhausted. After years of carrying responsibilities in an apparently insatiable institution, punctuated at regular intervals in some churches by new challenges, strategies, visions and programmes, they cannot sustain the pace any longer. Sometimes family or work demands precipitate a crisis. Sometimes burnout arrives before they detect the warning signs. Sometimes the questions become unanswerable. What is church for? How does church relate to the rest of my life? Why am I doing this? What would happen if I just stopped?

The institutional paraphernalia, administrative complexity, membership expectations and multiple activities that churches at the centre of a sacral society could sustain are inappropriate and burdensome for a marginal missionary movement.[8] One of the joys of emerging churches is the freedom not only to do things differently but to do fewer things. Simpler and more sustainable patterns release time and energy for 'being' as well as 'doing', friendships within and beyond the church and 'kingdom activities' as well as 'church activities'.[9] If church after Christendom is to be sustainable, it must be simple.

Simple, not simplistic

Talk of simplicity raises fears that church might become simplistic. This is, after all, why many people leave church. They find unpalatable its superficial relationships, infantile ethos, dependency culture, facile biblical interpretation and crass comments on social and cultural issues. This is not the kind of church Ephesians 4 envisages, in which members are no longer infants (v. 14), easily deceived or impressed by clever talk. But simple need not be simplistic. The components of churches worth joining and staying in that emerged in chapter 2 are not simplistic, but they are quite simple.[10]

Phrases such as 'a second naiveté' and 'simplicity beyond complexity' point towards the possibility of attaining a mature simplicity without becoming simplistic. James Fowler's 'faith development' model, mentioned earlier, proposes a similar trajectory.[11] Perhaps communities, as well as individuals, can achieve this mature simplicity. Some emerging churches become quite complex before

---

[8] See further Murray, *Post-Christendom*, 274–6.

[9] Although the institutional pull towards complicated, demanding and all-absorbing church life is hard to resist. Many young churches become busy, wear themselves out and fail to develop into healthy missional communities.

[10] See page 64.

[11] See page 50.

attaining a sustainable simplicity. Many inherited churches will need to discern what to discard and retain en route from the complexities of Christendom to the simplicity that will sustain marginal churches in post-Christendom.

Simplicity does not imply a 'back to basics' approach that entrenches inherited ways of doing things. Nor does it excuse us from careful and continuing engagement with the complex plurality of postmodern and post-Christendom culture. The diversity of missional and ecclesial responses needed will likely increase rather than decrease. Nor does it mean we can evade the challenge of moving beyond homogeneity to the more demanding challenge of crossing cultural boundaries and becoming mature disciples in churches that express unity through diversity. But sustainable responses to these challenges may themselves need to be relatively simple.

The essential components of church – mission, community and worship – need not be unduly complicated. Simplicity does not mean blandness, aesthetic poverty or lack of creativity; there are various ways of configuring these components. But some forms of church life will simply become unsustainable as churches become more marginal. And there is something authentic and deeply satisfying about the simplicity of church life in some areas of the world relatively untouched by Christendom. Some emerging and inherited churches, especially in poorer communities, have a similar ethos. One of the core values of *Urban Expression* in East London is 'uncluttered church'.[12]

Every so often we catch a glimpse of a simpler form of church. In September 2003 I drove straight from a Churches Together in England meeting I had been addressing to the small church community to which I belong on the edge of Oxford. I left behind an impressive array of

---

[12] See www.urbanexpression.org.uk.

archbishops, moderators, denominational leaders and ecumenical officers discussing all kinds of complex ecclesial issues. I arrived in time for a fish-and-chips supper, prayer around the table and passionate conversation about plans to demolish the old church building and replace it with homes for homeless men from a city-centre hostel. Both were expressions of church, but the simple one seemed just as authentic and, despite outward appearances, more sustainable.

The power of simplicity

Many writers suggest that churches are attractive and effective when they do simple things well. Church after Christendom will in this sense be no different from churches in other times and places.

Jeanne Hinton and Peter Price, for example, interpret in this way the attraction of the early churches:

> They demonstrated the power of God through their love for each other and their attention to the practice of forgiveness, confessing their sins, seeking to live their faith by kind actions, sincerity and neighbourliness, and being careful not to become anxious about tomorrow's problems. For some people this may not seem very revolutionary, but when we look at the things that divide human society, the diligent practice of such virtues becomes quite impressive.[13]

Many people have found Graham Tomlin's *The Provocative Church* a refreshing and challenging alternative to much recent writing on evangelism. He argues that churches must first provoke questions – by the way Chris-

---

[13] Jeanne Hinton and Peter Price, *Changing Communities* (London: CTBI, 2003), xvii. See further Kreider, *Worship*.

tians live and congregations operate – rather than trying to answer questions people have no incentive to ask.[14] Gracious but counter-cultural behaviour, healthy and honest relationships and worship that is both authentic and accessible may provoke questions, especially among those who belong before they believe. As the 'ethos gap' grows between church and post-Christendom culture, very simple and ordinary behaviour may be increasingly provocative.

But simple and ordinary Christian living is attractive and effective in all cultures. John Drane writes:

> The church is growing in the two-thirds world today largely through the unspectacular witness of ordinary Christians, often children and women. If we could bring ourselves to learn from them, that would be really good news, not only for the church but also for the wider culture.[15]

And Martin Robinson concludes:

> The acts of grace that most change the world consist of those actions that will never be widely publicised … No matter where in the world you look, those who have become Christians have overwhelmingly made such a decision because of the actions of ordinary people in their circle of influence.[16]

Marginal churches in post-Christendom will have fewer resources and less access to power and influence, but the church's heritage in many communities will present numerous opportunities to live out the good news. Ann Morisy

---

[14] Graham Tomlin, *The Provocative Church* (London: SPCK, 2002).

[15] John Drane, *Cultural Change and Biblical Faith* (Carlisle: Paternoster, 2000), 17.

[16] Robinson and Smith, *Invading*, 105.

reminds us that, even in post-Christendom, 'churches are still the most significant voluntary activity in Britain' and 'no other agency will have the voice and depth of history that the Church represents'.[17]

Interestingly, the local press is often favourable towards the involvement of churches in the local community, whilst the national press is much more hostile to the church as an institution. Maybe simple grass-roots activities will do more to restore the church's tarnished image and commend the story it tells than anything churches can say or do at a national level. Perhaps, too, powerless and marginal churches can rehabilitate the simple but derided notion of 'doing good', once people can no longer perceive this as the patronising beneficence of a dominant institution.

Ephesians 4 lists the virtues of a church on the way to maturity: humility, gentleness, patience, love and peace (vv. 2–3). These traits, the passage indicates, are not innate but need sustaining. They inspire and empower the unspectacular acts of kindness through which people discover the good news; but we need honest and healthy communities to nurture these simple virtues, train our reflexes, challenge inconsistent behaviour and sustain our vision.

Simplicity and hope

Church after Christendom is, finally, a community that sustains hope. For exiles in a strange new world, this is essential. Even those who enthusiastically celebrate the end of Christendom and the demise of imperialistic Christianity may fear for the future of church and society in postmodern Western culture.

Does the church have a future in Western culture? Can it adjust to life on the margins? Is this period of exile God's

---

[17] Morisy, *Journeying*, 58, 148.

judgement on the pretensions of Christendom? Has God then abandoned us? Or is there still hope? Has God rescued us from Christendom in order to bring a chastened and renewed church into a new future in Western culture?

Post-Christendom is a new environment. We have not been here before and do not know what the years ahead will hold. I find backward-looking prophecies of revival and unrealistic expectations of recovery unconvincing and irresponsible. We cannot be sure that there will *be* a church after Christendom in Western culture (although we remain confident in Jesus' promise that he will build his global church).

Ephesians 4 envisages a church united in hope (v. 4), confident in its destiny (v. 13) and getting on with the simple day-to-day business of speaking the truth in love (v. 15) and doing works of service (v. 12). If the church does survive the demise of Christendom, it will surely be a church sustained by simplicity and hope. Humble resilience, realistic expectations, modest ambitions, defiant prayers for God's kingdom, openness to the surprising grace of God and unshakable hope in the biblical promise that 'all the ends of the earth [even, one day, post-Christendom] will see the salvation of our God'[18] – these will sustain life and faith after Christendom.

And what of post-Christendom Western culture? What vision and values will hold it together? However much they differ, modernity and postmodernity both lack hope. Modernity anticipated progress towards a utopian future, but this future had no sense of purpose or ultimate meaning. Postmodernity is deeply sceptical about progress and scathing about ultimate meaning. But can human beings live without hope, without a story?

---

[18] Isaiah 52:10.

This, I believe, is the primary task of the church after Christendom – to offer hope humbly, graciously, gently and winsomely. Hope must be realistic, not triumphalistic. It must be sensitive to the pain and disorientation of the present as well as confident in God's future. It is hope rooted in the story of Israel and culminating in the story of Jesus – a story that the Christendom shift transmuted into just another imperial epic, but a story which marginal churches might just be able to recover and commend with sensitivity and integrity.

Select Bibliography

Anderson, Leith, *A Church for the 21st Century* (Grand Rapids: Bethany House, 1992)

Booker, Mike and Mark Ireland, *Evangelism – Which Way Now?: An Evaluation of Alpha, Emmaus, Cell Church and Other Contemporary Strategies for Evangelism* (London: Church House, 2003)

Brierley, Peter, *The Tide is Running Out: What the English Church Attendance Survey Reveals* (London: Christian Research, 2000)

Brown, Callum, *The Death of Christian Britain: Understanding Secularisation 1800–2000* (London: Routledge, 2001)

Bruce, Steve, *God is Dead: Secularization in the West* (Oxford: Blackwell, 2002)

Croft, Steven, *Transforming Communities: Re-imagining the Church for the 21st Century* (London: Darton, Longman & Todd, 2002)

Davie, Grace, *Religion in Britain since 1945: Believing without Belonging* (Oxford: Blackwell, 1994)

Drane, John, *The McDonaldization of the Church: Spirituality, Creativity, and the Future of the Church* (London: Darton, Longman & Todd, 2000)

Fanstone, Michael, *The Sheep That Got Away* (Tunbridge Wells: MARC, 1993)

Finney, John, *Finding Faith Today* (Swindon: Bible Society, 1992)

Frost, Michael and Alan Hirsch, *The Shaping of Things to Come: Innovation and Mission for the 21st Century Church* (Peabody: Hendrickson, 2004)

Gibbs, Eddie and Ian Coffey, *Church Next: Quantum Changes in Christian Ministry* (Leicester: Inter-Varsity Press, 2001)

Jamieson, Alan, *A Churchless Faith: Faith Journeys Beyond the Churches* (London: SPCK, 2002)

—, *Journeying in Faith* (London: SPCK, 2004)

Kelly, Gerard, *Retrofuture: Rediscovering Our Roots, Recharting Our Routes* (Downers Grove: InterVarsity Press, 1999)

Kreider, Alan, *Worship and Evangelism in Pre-Christendom* (Cambridge: Grove, 1995)

Lings, George, *Encounters on the Edge* (Sheffield: The Sheffield Centre, quarterly)

McLeod, Hugh and Werner Ustorf (eds.), *The Decline of Christendom in Western Europe, 1750–2000* (Cambridge: Cambridge University Press, 2003)

Mission-Shaped Church (London: Church House Publishing, 2004)

Morisy, Ann, *Journeying Out: A New Approach to Christian Mission* (London: Morehouse, 2004)

Moynagh, Michael, *Emergingchurch.intro* (Oxford: Monarch, 2004)

Murray, Stuart, *Post-Christendom* (Carlisle: Paternoster, 2004)

—, *Changing Mission: Learning from the Newer Churches* (London: CTBI, 2005)

Murray, Stuart and Anne Wilkinson-Hayes, *Hope from the Margins* (Cambridge: Grove, 1999)

Nazir-Ali, Michael, *Shapes of the Church to Come* (Eastbourne: Kingsway, 2001)

Pearse, Meic and Chris Matthews, *We must stop meeting like this …* (Eastbourne: Kingsway, 1999)

Richter, Philip and Leslie Francis, *Gone but not Forgotten: Church leaving and returning* (London: Darton, Longman & Todd, 1998)

Stuart, Morris, *So Long, Farewell and Thanks for the Church?* (London: Scripture Union, 1996)

Thomas, Richard, *Counting People In: Changing the way we think about membership and the church* (London: SPCK, 2003)

Thwaites, James, *Renegotiating the Church Contract: The Death and Life of the 21st Century Church* (Carlisle: Paternoster, 2001)

Warren, Robert, *Signs of Life: How Goes the Decade of Evangelism?* (London: Church House, 1996)

Webber, Robert, *Ancient-Future Faith: Rethinking Evangelicalism for a Postmodern World* (Grand Rapids: Baker, 1999)

Faith and Politics
After Christendom

The Church as a
Movement for Anarchy

Jonathan Bartley

For the best part of 1700 years, the institutional church has enjoyed a hand-in-hand relationship with government. Indeed, the church has often been seen as the glue that has stopped political systems from disintegrating into anarchy.

But now for the first time in centuries, the relationship has weakened to the point where the church in the UK can no longer claim to play any decisive part in Government. *Faith and Politics After Christendom* offers perspectives and resources for Christians and churches no longer at the centre of society but on the margins. It invites a realistic and hopeful response to challenges and opportunities awaiting the church in twenty-first century politics.

ISBN: 1-84227-348-5